ALAN BUSH: A SOURCE BOOK

ALAN BUSH

A SOURCE BOOK

compiled by

STEWART R. CRAGGS

780.92
B 9782 c

Published by
Ashgate Publishing Ltd
Gower House
Croft Road
Aldershot
Hants GU11 3HR
England

Ashgate Publishing Company
Suite 420
101 Cherry Street
Burlington, VT 05401–4405
USA

Ashgate website: http://www.ashgate.com

British Library Cataloguing in Publication Data
Alan Bush : a source book
 1.Bush, Alan Dudley, 1900–1995 2.Bush, Alan Dudley, 1900–1995 –
Bibliography 3.Composers – England
I.Craggs, Stewart R.
016.7'8'092

Library of Congress Cataloging-in-Publication Data
Craggs, Stewart R.
 Alan Bush : a source book / compiled by Stewart R. Craggs.
   p. cm.
 Includes bibliographical references (p.   ) and indexes.
 ISBN 978- 0-7546-0894-3 (alk. paper)
 1. Bush, Alan, 1900–1995—Bibliography. I. Title.

 ML134.B939C74 2007
 780.92—dc22

2006006944

ISBN 978-0-7546-0894-3

Printed on acid-free paper

Printed and bound in Great Britain by Antony Rowe Ltd, Chippenham

Contents

For

Cordelia and Tony

and my grandson

Ben

(born 22 April 2005)

Profile

Rachel O'Higgins

Alan Bush was born in Dulwich, London on 22 December 1900. His father, Alfred Walter Bush, was a director of the firm of W. J. Bush & Co., manufacturers of Fine Chemicals and Essential Oils, which had been founded about 1850, by his great-grandfather, William John Bush. His mother, Alice Maud Bush, was the daughter of George Brinsley, an estate agent. She was a talented artist at the Crystal Palace of Art, but her Victorian middle-class family discouraged her from pursuing a profession in either art or in medicine in which she was also interested. She married Alfred Bush and had three sons, Alan Bush being the youngest.

Alan Bush, delicate as a child, was educated at home until the age of eleven. He then went to Highgate School until the end of 1917. In January 1918, he entered the Royal Academy of Music and was a student there until the summer of 1922. He studied organ with Reginald Steggall, piano with Tobias Matthay and Lily West, and composition with Frederick Corder. While at the Academy, he received many awards – these included the Thalberg Scholarship for piano playing and the Battison Haynes and Philip Agnew Prizes for composition. After leaving the Royal Academy of Music, he studied piano with Benno Moiseivitch and Mabel Lander, both former pupils of Theodor Leschetizky, from whom he learnt the Leschetizky method. In the mid-1920s, he studied piano with Artur Schnabel in Berlin and from 1922 to 1927, he also studied composition with John Ireland. In 1925, he was appointed a Professor of Composition at the Royal Academy of Music, but was given leave of absence to pursue his studies in Berlin. In 1929, he entered the Friedrich-Wilhelm University in Berlin, studying philosophy and musicology. He also gave a number of piano and chamber recitals in Berlin, often of his own compositions. He intended to take a degree in philosophy and musicology, but with the onset of the Great Depression in 1929, he was obliged to return to London and resumed his professional musical life in 1931.

Early works include his *String Quartet in A Minor* (Opus 4), for which, in 1925, he won a Carnegie Award, and the *Five Pieces for Violin, Viola, Cello, Clarinet and Horn* (Opus 6). His quartet, *Dialectic*, (Opus 15) (1929), was another important work and composed in the form of a sonata; it is still regarded as one of his leading compositions and is one of Bush's best known works. His *Concert Piece for Cello and Piano* (Opus 17) (1936) was also regarded as a work of great maturity. *Dialectic* and the *Concert Piece* were performed at festivals of the International Society for Contemporary Music in Prague and Paris in the 1930s. In 1931, Bush resumed his position as Professor of Composition at the Royal Academy, and remained there until 1975, when he finally retired. In 1938, he was elected a Fellow of the Royal Academy of Music. He married Nancy Head, the sister of Michael Head, a singer and composer, in 1931 and later the same year returned permanently to Britain and settled in Radlett (Herfordshire). He had three daughters, though one was killed in a road accident in 1943.

In 1924, Bush joined the Independent Labour Party, though when the IIP disaffiliated from the Labour Party in 1929, he resigned from it and joined the Labour Party. In 1925, he became involved, along with Rutland Boughton, with the London Labour Choral Union and in 1929 became its Musical Advisor until the organisation collapsed in 1940. In 1936, he helped to found the Workers' Music Association. He became its first Chairman, until he was called up into the British Army in 1941, when he was elected its first President, a post he held until he died in 1995. Bush became the founder and conductor of the London String Orchestra in 1938, which continued with a break during the war until 1951. It was made up of many young, gifted string players of his day, such as Norman Brainin and Emanuel Hurwitz, who later made international careers.

In 1934, Bush wrote the music for a big theatrical pageant, *The Pageant of Labour*, held at the Crystal Palace, and conducted it with the assistance of Michael Tippett. In 1938, he was involved, as musical director, in two important musical events, a production of Handel's oratorio *Belshazzar* as an opera, and a huge pageant, at Wembley Stadium, staged by the London Co-operative Society. Finally, as a last effort before the outbreak of World War II in 1939, a *Festival of Music for the People*, ending with a Pageant, was held in the Albert Hall which was conducted by Bush and in which Paul Robeson took part. In 1935, Bush joined the Communist Party. Major works during this period include the *Piano Concerto*, (Opus 18) (1937), which was first performed in a BBC Contemporary Music concert on 4 March 1938, conducted by Sir Adrian Boult, with the composer as soloist. It later received three further performances, one on the Paris Radio with Margaret Kitchin as soloist, and two in London with Alan Bush conducting. As early as 1931, he had been commissioned by the BBC Wireless Military Band to write a work for them and he provided *Dance Overture*, later re-scored for symphony orchestra. In April and November 1940, he conducted two orchestral concerts at Queen's Hall in London, the programme including the first performances in Britain of Dmitri Shostakovich's *Symphony No. 5* (Opus 47), and Aram Khatchaturian's *Piano Concerto* with Moura Lympany as soloist. In March 1941, Bush was placed under a ban on his music and appearance in broadcasts by the BBC because he was one of the signatories of the People's Convention. This ban continued until 22 June, 1941, with the invasion by Hitler of the Soviet Union.

In November 1941, Bush was called up and entered the Royal Army Medical Service, where he became a reception clerk in the Outpatients' Department at Millbank Military Hospital, Chelsea. He spent most of his period of service in London, where he organised an army choir and was able to continue to conduct his London String Orchestra, which gave numerous broadcasts. In 1944, he played the piano part in the first performance in Great Britain of Shostakovich's Piano Quintet, with the Philharmonic String Quartet, led by Jean Pougnet. He was demobilised on 9 December 1945. Once the war was over, Bush again pursued his career as a composer, and teacher, which continued almost until he died in 1995.

During the war, he composed little, but *Lyric Interlude* (Opus 26) (1944), which was dedicated to his wife, is generally regarded as a lyrical work of high quality. Once he left the army, he began composing again, and one of his first works was a short cantata, *The Winter Journey* (Opus 29) (1946) with words by Randall Swingler. This was given its first performance at Alnwick Parish Church, Northumberland, and broadcast from there. He also wrote a children's opera, *The Press Gang*, to words by Nancy Bush. This was first performed at St. Christopher's School, Letchworth in 1947, and was later televised with Watford Children's Co-operative Choir. In 1947-48, Alan Bush was Chairman of the Composers' Guild of Great Britain, and its Treasurer during 1956-57.

Alan Bush has more than one hundred orchestral, instrumental and vocal works to his credit, together with four full length operas, *Wat Tyler*, *Men of Blackmoor*, *The Sugar Reapers* (entitled Guyana Johnny when it was performed in Leipzig) and *Joe Hill: The Man Who Never Died*. The libretti of the first three were by Nancy, his wife, and the libretto of the fourth was by an American playwright, Barrie Stavis. *Wat Tyler*, which received a prize in the Arts Council Opera Competition in 1951, was performed at Sadler's Wells Theatre in 1974 to very great acclaim. *Men of*

Blackmoor was performed by the Oxford University Opera Society and the Bristol University Opera Society, but has never had a professional production in this country. The world premiere of *Wat Tyler* was in Leipzig on 6 September, 1953, that of *Men of Blackmoor* on 18 November, 1956. *The Sugar Reapers* was also first performed in Leipzig on 14 December 1966 and *Joe Hill* on 29 September, 1970 in Berlin. There were broadcasts of *Wat Tyler*, *Men of Blackmoor* and *Joe Hill* by the BBC and by the Radio of the German Democratic Republic. All four operas were staged on the Continent, in particular, in the German Democratic Republic and received more than twenty productions over a period of years from the 1950s until the 1970s.

The *Three Concert Studies for Piano Trio* (Opus 31) which were composed in 1947, were inspired by Bulgarian folk melodies.

Other works of note include his *Violin Concerto* (Opus 32) (1949), which was dedicated to Max Rostal, who gave its first performance at a Promenade Concert on 25 August 1949. The cantata *Voices of the Prophets* (Opus 41 (1953) was commissioned by Peter Pears in 1952, and sung by him with Noel Mewton Wood at the piano at the first performance in the Recital Room, Royal Festival Hall on 22 March 1953. Instrumental works include the *Dorian Pasacalia and Fugue for Orchestra,* (Opus 52) (1959), which had its first performance at the Cheltenham Festival, July 1961 and *Variations, Nocturne and Finale on an English Sea-Song for Piano and Orchestra*, (Opus 60), which was also performed at the Cheltenham Festival, on 7 July 1964 with David Wilde playing the piano. During the winter of 1971-2, Bush composed his *Concert Overture for an Occasion,* (Opus 74). The occasion was the 150th anniversary of the RAM, the institution he was associated with for fifty years. Throughout his life, he composed many songs both for the labour choirs he conducted, for Welsh male voice choirs and to commemorate certain events. For example, he wrote a beautiful song with words by Nancy Bush to commemorate the destruction of Lidice by the Nazis during World War II - *Lidice* for unaccompanied mixed chorus (1947). He even wrote a song to commemorate the first journey into space by Yuri Gagarin, *Song of the Cosmonaut*, in 1961.

Alan Bush also wrote four symphonies, the first of which was *Symphony No. 1 in C* (Opus 21) which was first performed at a Promenade Concert on 24 July 1942, conducted by the composer. This was followed by the *Nottingham Symphony* (Opus 33) (1949), which received its first performance in the Albert Hall, Nottingham and was conducted by David Ellenberg. It was commissioned by the Co-operative Society to commemorate the 500th Anniversary of the City Charter. Sir Adrian Boult conducted its first London performance at the Royal Festival Hall on 11 December 1952 with the London Philharmonic Orchestra. The third symphony, the *Byron Symphony* (Opus 53) (1959), with baritone solo and mixed choir was first performed in Leipzig on March 22, 1962 and its first British performance was in London in the Festival Hall on 6 June 1962. His final symphony, the *Lascaux Symphony* (Opus 98) was completed in the early 1980s. It was inspired by a visit to the Lascaux caves in France where Bush saw the original cave paintings.

In 1968, he became a Doctor of Music of London University, and in 1970, the Doctorate of Music (Honoris Causa) was conferred upon him by Durham University. He lived in Radlett from 1932 until his death in 1995. He had a very contented home life, being happily married to his wife, Nancy, who collaborated with him both as librettist for three of his operas and as writer of lyrics for numerous songs.

Reproduced by kind permission

Acknowledgements

I owe a great debt of gratitude to Dr Rachel O'Higgins and her husband Professor Paul O'Higgins for their help and kindnesses over the years and for welcoming me into their home on numerous occasions while the present volume was being prepared.

I also owe a debt of gratitude to Dr Nicolas Bell, Curator of the Music Collections at the British Library, for his help with Alan Bush's manuscripts and letters, and reading drafts of this volume.

I should also like to thank Dr Jane Birkett, archivist at the Theatre Museum, Dr Timothy Bowers (Royal Academy of Music), Michael Hinson for supplying details of the Bush family tree, Professor John Dressler of Murray State University, Kentucky USA, Jaime Harris-Hughes, Archivist, Nottinghamshire Archives, Mrs Linda McGowen, Dr. John B. Marsden, Sally Banham and Cat Smith of Nottingham Central Library, Bridgit Palmer, Special Collections Librarian at the Royal Academy of Music, Jacquie Kavanagh and Jeff Walden of the BBC's Written Archive Centre at Caversham, and John Jeffrey, archivist of the Workers' Music Association.

Finally, I am very grateful to Rachel Lynch, Heidi May and Ellen Keeling at Ashgate Publishing for their help and guidance with this book.

Index of titles

Guyana Johnny, *see* The Sugar Reapers

Here they lie that once had breath, *see* Songs of the Doomed (Opus 14)
(A) Heart's Expression for Piano (Opus 121), 128
Himavirdani Râga, *see* Three Râga Melodies (Opus 59)
Hiroshima: Incidental Music, 76
His War or Yours: Ballet (1935), 43
Homage to William Sterndale Bennett (Opus 27), 64-5
(The) Hope Concealed, *see* Freedom on the Air
Hush be still you bitter thing, *see* Songs of the Doomed (Opus 14)

Ice Age Remembered, *see* Symphony No. 4 (Opus 98)
(The) Ice Breaks, *see* Freedom on the Air (1940)
Il Palazzo Savioli, *see* Symphony No. 3 (Opus 53)
Introduction and Dance-Duet (Opus 78, No. 2), 109
Invention for two voices, *see* Six Short Pieces for Piano (Opus 99)
Islay Reaper's Song, *see* Compass Points (Opus 83)
It's Up to Us, 131

Jack the Jolly Tar, *see* Four Seafarers' Songs (Opus 57)
(The) Jacket-Makers' Song, *see* Songs of Asian Struggle
Joe Hill: The Man Who Never Died, ix, 22, 97-8
Joseph's Narration (1946), 62-3
(The) Journey, *see* The Winter Journey (Opus 29)
(The) Joy of Harvest, *see* Songs of Asian Struggle

Keep (The), *see* Piers Plowman's Day (Opus 30)
Kinloch Iorram, *see* Suite for Two Pianos (Opus 65)

Labour's Song of Challenge for Chorus and Piano, 44
(The) Lake Isle of Innisfree, *see* Two Songs (Yeats),
(The) Last Days of Pompeii: opera (1923), 30
Learning to Talk: song for mixed chorus, 131
Learning to Talk, *see* Life's Span (Opus 77)
Leave Your Brains in Bed, *see* Freedom on the Air (1940)
Letter Galliard for Piano (Opus 80), 110-11
Lidice for Unaccompanied Chorus, x, 68-9
Life's Span: Song Cycle (Opus 77), 109-10
Like as the Waves make towards the Pebbled Shore, *see* Two
  Shakespeare Sonnets (Opus 92)
Like Rivers Flowing: Part Song for Mixed Chorus, 86

Chronology

1829

9 January   William John Bush (grandfather) born in Hackney
                   (died 1889). Manufacturing chemist and distiller of
                   essential oils. Company founded in 1851

1832

31 August   Mary Ann Yarroll (grandmother) born in Hackney

1854

21 October   Marriage of William and Mary at St. Leonard's
                   Church, Shoreditch

1863

13 May   Alice Maud Brinsley (mother) born in Newington,
                   London (died 13 April 1951)

1865

17 November   Alfred Walter Bush (father) born in Hackney (died
                   13 August 1935), the eighth of 13 children who
                   became MD of W.J. Bush & Co.

1894

18 January   Marriage of Alfred and Alice at St. Paul's Church,
                   Forest Hill, London

| 13 December | Birth of Alfred John (first son) at "Lordship Lane, SE" |

1896

| 30 May | Birth of Hamilton Brinsley (second son) at Lordship Lane (died 10 November 1953) |

1900

| 22 December | Alan Dudley (third son) born at Bridge House, Lordship Lane |

1907

| 11 March | Birth of Nancy Rachel Head |

1911-1917 | Educated at Sir Roger Cholmeley's Grammar School, Highgate where in 1916-1917, he was a Foundation Scholar. Passed the London Matriculation in 1917 |

1917

| 31 July | Alfred Bush, a 2nd Lieutenant serving with the 2nd Lincolnshire Regiment, is killed in action. His name is recorded on Panel 21 of the Menin Gate Memorial at Ypres |

1918

| January | Enters the Royal Academy of Music and studies organ with Reginald Steggall, piano with Tobias Matthay and Lily West and composition with Frederick Corder |

| 13 April | The Royal College of Heralds grant a family crest to Alfred W. Bush |

| 15 June | Plays the Andante Presto from his *Sonata in G for* |

Violin and Piano with Gladys Chester at a RAM Concert

1919

1 February	Warwick Braithwaite plays his *Variations on an Original Theme* for piano at a RAM Fortnightly Concert
3 February	Plays the first movement of Rheinberger's *Organ Sonata in D minor* at a RAM Organ Recital in the Duke's Hall
29 March	Awarded the Charles Mortimer Prize at the RAM
31 May	Plays Beethoven's *Andante in F* at a RAM Fortnightly Concert
28 June	Plays his *Variations on an Original Theme* at a concert in the Wigmore Hall, London ("Lily West and her pupils")
15 July	Plays his *Variations on an Original Theme* at a RAM Scholars Concert
18 December	Plays Weber's *Moto Perpetuo* at a Wigmore Hall Invitation Concert ("Lily West and her pupils")

1920

24 January	Plays Arnold Bax's *Dream in Exile* for piano at a RAM Fortnightly Concert
10 March	Plays Chopin's *Fantasie-Polonaise* at a RAM Student's Chamber Concert in the Duke's Hall
July	Awarded the Oliveria Prescott Gift at the RAM (Miniature scores of Beethoven's 9 Symphonies)
3 July	Plays his *Sonata in E for Violin and Piano* with Florence Lockwood at a RAM concert

5 July	The above is repeated at a RAM Students's Chamber Concert and reported in the *Daily Telegraph* the following day
15 July	Plays Medtner's *Tragedy Fragment in G minor* (Opus 7), partly with Lily West, at a RAM Scholars Concert
17 November	Plays the second and third movements of J.S. Bach's *Italian Concerto* at a RAM Students' Chamber Concert in the Duke's Hall. A note in the programme describes Bush as a Thalberg Scholar, an award received for piano playing at the RAM
December	Receives the Battison Haynes Prize for composition at the RAM
17 December	Gives a piano recital at the Wigmore Hall. John Ireland's *Sonata in E minor* is included in the programme

1921

2 March	Plays his *Three Pieces for Two Pianos* with Reginald Paul at a Students' Chamber Concert, Royal Academy of Music
May	Receives The Philip L. Agnew Composition Prize at the RAM. It is signed by Arnold Bax
10 May	Plays his *Sonata for Piano in B minor* at a Lyceum Club Concert. This was repeated at a Students' Chamber Concert on 6 July at the Royal Academy

1922

1 March	Plays J.S. Bach's *Concerto in C major* for two pianos at a RAM Students' Chamber Concert

7 June	Receives the Matthew Philimore Prize for piano playing
	Becomes an Associate of the Royal Academy and studies composition with John Ireland (until 1927). Also studies piano with Benno Moiseivich and Mabel Lander
20 June	Plays Michael Head's (his future brother-in-law) *Concerto for piano and string orchestra* at a Students' Orchestral Concert, conducted by Sir Alexander Mackenzie
1924	Joins the Independent Labour Party
May	Starts to compose the *Piano Quartet* (Opus 5) which is completed in March 1925
1925	Wins a Carnegie Award for his *String Quartet in A minor* (Opus 4)
	Appointed as Professor of Harmony and Composition at the Royal Academy of Music (until 1978)
1926	Becomes actively involved in the London Labour Choral Union as Assistant Musical Director
26 May	Starts to compose *Symphonic Impression* (Opus 8) which is completed in February 1927
1927	
24 May	The *Piano Quartet* (Opus 5) is included in a concert of unpublished works by members of the Faculty of Music, organised by Arthur Bliss
December	Starts to compose *Song To the Men of England* which is completed in January 1928

1928	Visits Berlin
February	Completes composition of *Relinquishment* for piano (Opus 11)
1929	Resigned from the Independent Labour Party and joined the Labour Party
	Studies philosophy and musicology in Berlin until 1931
	Appointed Musical advisor to London Labour Choral Union, and conductor in succession to Rutland Boughton
September/October	Completes composition of *Dance Overture* (Opus 12)
30 November	Gives a concert in Berlin where he plays Bach, Ireland and Beethoven
1931	
31 March	Marries Nancy Rachel Head at Paddington Register Office. Returns to Berlin and studies with Artur Schnabel for the rest of the year
1932	
February	Starts to compose *Songs of the Doomed* (Opus 14) which are completed in March 1933
20 May	Birth of eldest daughter, Rachel Elizabeth
	Appointed as an examiner to the Associated Board of the Royal Schools of Music, London
1934	Meets Gerhard and Hanns Eisler, Ernst Meyer and Georg Knepler in London

15-20 October	Conducts (with Michael Tippett) the *Pageant of Labour* at Crystal Palace
22 November	Plays two of his compositions at a RAM New Music Society concert
1935	Joins the Communist Party of Great Britain
1936	Co-founder of the Workers' Music Association
8 March	Conducts the premiere of Benjamin Britten's *Russian Funeral* at the Westminster Theatre in London
May-September	Composes the *Concert Piece* for cello and piano (Opus 17)
6 June	Birth of twin daughters, Catherine Brinsley and Alice Jennifer
	Starts to compose the *Piano Concerto* (Opus 18) which is finished on 22 December 1937
1937	
21 June	Performs the *Concert Piece* (Opus 17) at a ISCM concert in Paris
1938	Establishes and conducts the London String Orchestra (until 1952)
	Elected a Fellow of the Royal Academy of Music
16-21 May	Artistic director of a production of Handel's oratorio *Belshazzar*, staged as an opera, at the Scala Theatre in London
22 May	First WMA Anniversary Festival of Choral Music and Drama held in London

2 July	Conducts part of the *Pageant of Co-operation* at Wembley
October	Visits Moscow to meet Soviet artists (reported in *Izvestia,* 15 October 1938)
November	Visits the United States, with his wife and meets Aaron Copland, Charles Lomax and various refugees including Hanns Eisler
1939	Takes MusBac examinations at London University
30 January	First concert by the London String Orchestra at the Wigmore Hall
4 February	Addresses a conference in Peckham on the role of music and play in the co-operative movement
1 April	Organises and conducts *A Festival of Music for the People*, a pageant at the Royal Albert Hall, London
June	Starts to compose *Symphony No.1* (Opus 21) which is completed in August 1940
1940	
17 February	Second concert by the London String Orchestra
13 April	Conducts the London Philharmonic Orchestra in a concert of modern Russian music at Queen's Hall, London under the auspices of the Society for Cultural Relations with the USSR
1941	WMA Singers formed (in place of the London Labour Choral Union) Becomes President of the Workers' Music Association (until 1995) Also forms the William Morris Musical Society
12 January	Supports the Peoples' Convention for a People's Government with others including Michael Redgrave

| March-June | The BBC bans Bush's music as a result of his support of the People's Convention |
| November | Serves in the Royal Army Medical Corps for the remainder of World War II (until December 1945) |

1942

20 June	Conducts at a pageant ("An Agreement of the Peoples") held in London at Empress Hall (Earls Court) to mark the first anniversary of the German attack on the USSR
22 June	An exhibition is opened by Agnes Maisky, wife of the Soviet ambassador to the UK
24 July	Conducts his *Symphony No.1* (Opus 21) at a Promenade Concert with the BBC Symphony Orchestra

1943

21 June-4 July	A Soviet Music Exhibition is held at 160 Wardour Street, London where Bush undertakes tours and speaks about Russian music. *A Handbook of Soviet Composers*, edited by Bush, is published by Pilot Press
27 June	Conducts at a British-Soviet Unity Demo at the Royal Albert Hall
29 August	Completes work on *Resolution* (Opus 25)

1944

| September-October | Composes the *Lyric Interlude* for violin and piano (Opus 26) |

1945

| 6 January | Concert of Bush's music played by the London Philharmonic Orchestra |

1946	Appointed conductor of the WMA Singers (until 1956)
7-14 July	His *Symphony No. 1* is chosen for submission to the 20th ISCM Festival held in London
29 November	Conducts a concert of Czech music at the Wigmore Hall
1947	
January	Tours Yugoslavia and Bulgaria and conducts several works
October- November	Visits Czechoslovakia and Poland
1948	His *Strict Counterpoint in Palestrina Style* is published by Joseph Williams
	Starts to compose the *Violin Concerto* (Opus 32) which is completed in 1949. Also commissioned for a Symphony to mark the 500th Anniversary of the City of Nottingham
1949	Chairman of the Composers' Guild of Great Britain
27 June	The *Nottingham Symphony* is first performed in the Albert Hall, Nottingham
25 August	The *Violin Concerto* is first performed at a Henry Wood Promenade Concert
28 December	*The Press Gang* is televised by the BBC from Alexandra Palace with Bush conducting
1950	
15 December	The WMA give a 50th birthday concert in Conway Hall. A "Tribute to Alan Bush on his 50th Birthday" is also published by the WMA

1951	Visits Berlin
	Wins the Arts Council prize for the Festival of Britain Competition for *Wat Tyler*
1953	
5 January	A 50th Birthday Concert of works by composers who studied with Alan Bush is held at the Wigmore Hall in London
6 September	World premiere of *Wat Tyler* in Leipzig
1955	
26 March	Adjudicates at Ebbw Vale's 4th Annual Eisteddfod
1 May	Conducts *Salute to May Day*, a festival gala concert, organised by the British Workers' Sports Association at the Adelphi Theatre in London
29 September	Reveals in a letter that "I've finished the last page of the full score [of *Men of Blackmoor*]"
1956	Treasurer of the Composers' Guild of Great Britain for one year
18 November	World premier of *Men of Blackmoor* in Weimar
1958	
19 September	Attends the Commemoration Service for Ralph Vaughan Williams with Nancy in Westminster Abbey, London
1959	Starts to compose *Symphony No.3* (Opus 53)
August	Visits Guyana with Rachel, having previously been banned from entering the country in 1957

1961

14 June   The *Dorian Passacaglia and Fugue* is first
performed at the Cheltenham Festival

13 July   Major Yuri Gagarin autographs the score of *Song
of the Cosmonaut* on a visit to London

1962   Wins the Handel Prize for *Symphony No.3*,
Halle, German Democratic Republic

11 November   Informs Michael Tippett (in a letter) that he has
begun to compose *The Sugar Reapers*

1965

7 July   *Variations, Nocturne and Final on an English Sea
Song* first performed at the Cheltenham Festival

1966

2 January   Featured on BBC Radio 3 in the "Composer's
Portrait" series

11 December   World premiere of *The Sugar Reapers* in Leipzig

1968   Receives a Doctor of Music degree from the
University of London

1969

12 August   Presents a paper on the "National character an
essential ingredient in musical art today" to the
International Folk Music Council

1970   Awarded a Doctor of Music (Honoris Causa)
degree from the University of Durham

29 September   World premiere of *Joe Hill* in Berlin

| 6 December | BBC TV televise a programme about Bush to celebrate his 70th birthday |

1971

| 16 February | A 70th birthday celebration concert is given at the RAM |

| 30 April | A 70th birthday celebration concert is given at the College of Music, University of Cape Town |

1972

| 28 May | Ronald Stevenson gives the first performance of the *Piano Sonata in Ab* at the Bath Festival |

1974

| 19 June | Keynote Opera Society presents *Wat Tyler* at the Sadler's Wells Theatre in London |

1975

| 25 October | Bush is featured in a BBC programme "Born in 1900" |

| 6 November | First performance in England of *The Ballad of Freedom's Soldier* |

| 10 November | The RAM Club give a concert to celebrate the 50th anniversary of Bush's professorship at the RAM |

1976

| 11 January | The WMA gives a concert at the Wigmore Hall in honour of its president's 75th birthday |

1977

| 30 October | A concert of Bush's works is given at the Wigmore Hall |

1979

17 December   BBC Radio 3 broadcast a concert of Bush's works
                         from its Maida Vale Studios

1980   *In my Eighth Decade and Other Essays* is
                         published by Kahn & Averill

11 December   80th birthday concert from the British Music
                         Information Centre

21 December   80th birthday concert held in East Germany

22 December   80th birthday concert at Birmingham Museum and
                         Art Gallery
                         The BBC broadcast an 80th birthday tribute

1981

17 January   The WMA 80th birthday concert

31 March   Celebrates his 50th wedding anniversary.
                         A setting of *Two Shakespeare Sonnets* (Opus 92)
                         for Nancy, to mark the occasion, are dated 16/9/80

18 June   Concert of Bush's music at the Aldeburgh Festival

22 August   The WMA (Watford branch) hold a concert of
                         Poetry and Music by Nancy and Alan Bush

1983

17 February   Completes *A Song from the North* (Opus 97)

27 May   Completes composition of *Symphony No .4*
                         (Opus 98)

1984

19 February   Takes part in a BBC Radio 3 programme, "A
                         Portrait of Arnold Bax"

1986

10 January	An 85th birthday concert is held at the Queen Elizabeth Hall in London
12 January	Anna Ambrose's film "Alan Bush: A Life" is shown on Channel 4
25 March	First performance of *Symphony No .4* ("The Lascaux Symphony") by the BBC Philharmonic Orchestra

1991

12 October	Death of Nancy Bush, age 84

1995

31 October	Death of Alan Bush, age 94

1997

October	The Alan Bush Music Trust is formed "to promote the education and appreciation by the public in and of music, and, in particular the works of the British composer Alan Bush (1900-1995)"

2000

1 November	A Centenary Concert is held at the Wigmore Hall, London
2 November	An exhibition about his life and work is opened

Catalogue of works

Compositions are arranged chronologically. The information supplied about each includes, wherever possible, the following:

1. The title of the work with opus number
2. Text(s) used and details about the authors of texts
3. The body or person responsible for a work's commission
4. The required performing forces
5. Dedication
6. Duration
7. First performance(s)
8. Publication details
9. Details of the manuscript
10. Recordings
11. Bibliography (items arranged alphabetically by title)
12. Notes

1918

SONATA in G
For violin and piano

First performance of only the 'Andante Presto': London, Royal
  Academy of Music, 15 June 1918
  Gladys Chester (violin) and Alan Bush (piano)
Unpublished
Manuscript: Whereabouts unknown

1919

VARIATIONS ON AN ORIGINAL THEME
For piano

First performance: London, Royal Academy of Music, 1 February 1919
  Warwick Braithwaite (piano)
First (public) performance: London, Wigmore Hall, 28 June 1919
  Alan Bush (piano) at a 'Lily West and Her Pupils' concert
Unpublished
Manuscript: Whereabouts unknown
Bibliography: *The Times*, 29 June 1919, 15 (Anon.)

1920

SONATA in E minor
For violin and piano

First performance: London, Royal Academy of Music, 3 July 1920
  Florence Lockwood (violin) and Alan Bush (piano)
  Repeated at a students' concert, RAM, 5 July 1920
Unpublished
Manuscript: Whereabouts unknown
Bibliography: *The Daily Telegraph*, 6 July 1920, 8 (Anon.)

1921

THREE PIECES (Opus 1)
For two pianos

1. On the Warpath (Vigorous – Rhythmic)
2. Pastoral Scene (Slow)
3. At the Cinema (Allegro vivace)

Duration: 11′
First performance: London, Duke's Hall (Royal Academy of Music),
  2 March 1921. Alan Bush and Reginald Paul (pianos)
Publication: Murdoch, Murdoch & Co. Score © 1922
Manuscript: Whereabouts unknown
Bibliography: *Musical Times*, 62 (April 1921), 281 (Anon.); *Musical Times*, 62 (October 1921), 709 (H.G.)
Note: This work received the Charles Mortimer Prize

OTHER VERSIONS

At the Cinema
Arranged for solo piano
Publication: Murdoch, Murdoch, & Co. Score © 1922

SONATA No. 1 in B MINOR (Opus 2)
For piano in one continuous movement

Allegro deciso-Darkly-Andante-tranquillo-Piu moto e poco accelerando

Dedication: "To Philip L. Agnew"
Duration: 22′
First performance: London, Lyceum Club, 10 May 1921
  Alan Bush (piano)
  Repeated at a students' concert, RAM, 6 July 1921
Publication: Murdoch, Murdoch & Co. Score © 1923
Manuscript: Whereabouts unknown
Bibliography: *Musical Opinion*, 46 (August 1923), 1027 (Anon.); *Musical
  Times*, 64 (October 1923), 709 (Anon.)
Note: This work received the Philip L. Agnew Prize in May 1921

1922

FESTIVAL MARCH
For chamber orchestra
The 5th contribution to 'A Wreath of A Hundred Roses': An Occasional
Masque devised by Louis Napoleon Parker and written to mark the
Centenary Celebrations of the Royal Academy of Music
Commissioned by: The Royal Academy of Music

Instrumentation: 2 cornets in Bb, 2 horns, timpani, percussion (2), strings
  and organ

Duration: c. 5′
First performance: London, Queen's Hall, 17 July 1922
  The RAM Orchestra, conducted by Frederick Corder
Unpublished
Manuscript: London, Royal Academy of Music, MS 1744: Full score
  in ink
Bibliography: *Musical Times*, 63 (August 1922), 579-580 ("M"); *The*

Times, 12 July 1922, 11 (Anon.); *The Times*, 19 July 1922, 12 (Anon.)

1923

THE LAST DAYS OF POMPEII
Opera with libretto by Hamilton Brinsley Bush (Alan's brother) based on the novel by Edward Bulwer-Lytton

Instrumentation: In short score only
First (private) performance: Highgate (North London), c.1923
  Brinsley Bush (tenor), May Murphy (soprano) and Dorothy
  Giles (mezzo-soprano) with Alan Bush (piano)
Unpublished
Manuscript: Whereabouts unknown. Destroyed by the composer
Bibliography: Michael Head "Alan Bush as a fellow student" *in*
  Stevenson, R. (ed.), Time Remembered Alan Bush: an 80th
  birthday symposium. Kidderminster, Bravura, 1981, 69

PHANTASY in C minor (Opus 3)
For violin and piano
In three movements

1. Andante poco maestoso – Allegro giocoso
2. Andante sostenuto
3. Tempo primo – Allegro giocoso

Commissioned by: W.W. Cobbett
Duration: 10'15"
First (private) performance: London, The Studios (Wigmore Street), 10
  May 1924
  Evelyn Cooke (violin) and Alan Bush (piano)
First public performance: Hampstead (London), Town Hall, 4 December
  1924
  Florence Lockwood (violin) and Alan Bush (piano)
Unpublished
Manuscript: Whereabouts unknown
Recordings: Dutton CDLX 7130 (2002)
  N. Liddell (violin) and P. Fowke (piano)

PRISCILLA'S PAVANE
For cello with piano accompaniment

First performance: Unable to trace
Unpublished
Manuscript: British Library, London. MS. Mus. 366, ff. 57-59:
  Score and cello part in blue ink

1923-1924

QUARTET IN A MINOR FOR TWO VIOLINS, VIOLA AND VIOLONCELLO (Opus 4)
In three movements

1. Andante tranquillo
2. Presto
3. Andante sostenuto-Allegro vivace

Dedication: "To my mother"
Duration: 20′
First performance: Hampstead (London), Town Hall, 4 December 1924
  The Spencer Dyke String Quartet
First broadcast performance: London, BBC Studios, 11 June 1925
  The Virtuoso Quartet
Publication: Stainer and Bell & Co. Full score © 1925 (Part of the
  'Carnegie Collection of British Music')
Manuscript: Whereabouts unknown
Bibliography: *The Times*, 18 April 1925, 8 (Anon.); *The Times*, 25
  October 1926, 23 (Anon.)
Note: This work received the Carnegie United Kingdom Trust Award in
  1925

OTHER VERSIONS

Second movement arranged for String Orchestra entitled "Scherzo"

First performance: Ilford, Savoy Cinema, 25 July 1943
  The London String Orchestra, conducted by Alan Bush
Unpublished

1924-1925

QUARTET FOR PIANO, VIOLIN, VIOLA AND CELLO (Opus 5)
In three movements

1. Con moto moderato [12'11"]
2. Allegro vivace [6'56"]
3. Andante tranquillo, Allegro non troppo [10'34"]

First performance (movements 1 and 2): Hampstead (London), Town
   Hall, 4 December 1924
   Alan Bush and members of the Spencer Dyke String Quartet
First complete performance: London, Faculty of Arts Gallery (Upper John
   Street), 21 June 1927
   Alan Bush (piano) with John Pennington (violin), James Lockyer
   (viola) and Anthony Pini (cello) (Programme arranged by Arthur
   Bliss)
First broadcast performance: London, BBC Studios, 15 July 1933
   Alan Bush (piano) and the Brosa String Quartet
Unpublished
Manuscript: British Library, London. MS. Mus. 350 (ff. 107): Score in ink,
   with deletions in red crayon. Dated May 1924-March 1925.
Recordings: Dutton CDLX 7130 (2002). The London Piano Quartet
Bibliography: *The Times*, 24 June 1927, 14 (Anon.)

REVISED VERSION (1928)

First performance: Berlin, Bechsteinsall, 6 November 1928
   Alan Bush (piano) and members of the Brosa Quartet

1925-1926

FIVE PIECES FOR VIOLIN, VIOLA, CELLO, CLARINET AND HORN
   (Opus 6)

1. Lento
2. Allegro vivace
3. Allegretto comodo
4. Lento
5. Molto moderato ma deciso

Dedication: "To John Ireland"

Duration: 18'
First performance: Berlin, Bechsteinsall, 6 November 1928
  Antonio Brosa (violin), Leonard Rubens (viola), Anthony Pini
  (cello), Carl Essberger (clarinet) and Ernst Friese (horn)
First UK (broadcast) performance: London, BBC Studios, 17 June 1929
  Samuel Kutcher (violin), Bernard Shore (viola), Douglas
  Cameron (cello), Haydn Draper (clarinet) and Aubrey Brain (horn)
First UK concert performance: London, Armitage House (Great Portland
  Street), 29 January 1930
  Antonio Brosa (violin), Leonard Rubens (viola), Anthony Pini
  (cello), Haydn Draper (clarinet) and A.D. Hyde (horn)
  (A British Music Society Concert)
Unpublished
Manuscript: British Library, London. MS. Mus. 351 (ff. 202): Score and
  parts in ink. Dated March 1925-January 1926. The clarinet and
  horn parts are signed by the performers at the first performance

OTHER VERSIONS

Arrangement for wind and strings
by the composer

Unpublished

1926

TWO SONGS FOR SOPRANO AND CHAMBER ORCHESTRA (Opus 7)

1.   The Moth (Walter de la Mare) (Andante von moto)
2.   Overheard on a Saltmarsh (Harold Munro) (Lento)

1.0+1.1.1/2.0.0.0/harp and strings
Duration: 8'
First performance: Unable to trace
Unpublished
Manuscript: British Library, London. MS. Mus.416, 1-ff. 1-13; 2-ff. 14-27
  Dated February 1926 and March 1926

TWO SONGS
for voice and piano
Text: W.B. Yeats

1. The Lake Isle of Innisfree (tranquillo)
2. Down by the Salley Gardens (tranquillo)

First performance (No. 1): London, Rudolf Steiner Hall, 15 June 1927
  Hortense Houghton (soprano) and Alan Bush (piano)
First broadcast performance (No. 2): London, BBC Studios,
  25 August 1933. George Parker (baritone). No pianist is
  billed in *Radio Times* so accompaniment may have been
  provided by the BBC Orchestra, conducted by Victor Hely-
  Hutchinson
Unpublished
Manuscript: British Library, London. MS. Mus. 425, 1-ff. 1-6; 2-ff. 7-9:
  Score in ink. Dated March 1926
Bibliography: *The Times*, 17 June 1927, 12 (Anon.)

SONG TO LABOUR
For mixed chorus (SATB) and piano
Text: Charlotte Perkin Gilman

First performance: Unable to trace
Publication: Workers' Music Association. Vocal score © 1926
  Included in *Twelve Labour Choruses* (ILP [© 1930])
  Also published in Moscow (with Russian text) © 1963
Manuscript: Whereabouts unknown

1926-1927

SYMPHONIC IMPRESSION (Opus 8)
For orchestra

3.3.3.2/4.3.3.1/timpani/percussion(2)/strings

Duration: 18′
First (private) performance: London, Royal College of Music, 15
  November 1929
  Royal College of Music Orchestra, conducted by Alan Bush
  (A Patron's Fund Rehearsal)
First public performance: London, Queen's Hall, 11 September 1930
  BBC Symphony Orchestra, conducted by Alan Bush
  (A Henry Wood Promenade Concert: Broadcast by the BBC in the
  National Programme)
Unpublished

Manuscript: British Library, London. MS. Mus. 326, ff. 1-132: Full score
in ink. Dated 26 May-2 February
Bibliography: Programme notes for the first performance (DMC);
The Sunday Times, 14 September 1930, 5 (E. Newman); *The
Sunday Times*, 21 September 1930, 5 (E. Newman); *The Times*,
12 September 1930, 10 (Anon.)

OTHER VERSIONS

Arrangement for piano duet
by the composer

First performance: London, Faculty of Arts Gallery, 21 June 1927
Alan Bush and William Busch (piano)
Unpublished
Manuscript: British Library, London. MS. Mus. 326, ff. 133-161: Score in
ink with a draft score (also in ink) of portions of the second part.
Bibliography: *The Times*, 24 June 1927, 14 (Anon.)

1927

PRELUDE AND FUGUE (Opus 9)
For piano

Dedication: "To Edward J. Dent Esq". [in the printed score only]
Duration: 11'
First performance: London, Rudolf Steiner Hall, 15 June 1927
Alan Bush (piano)
First European performance: Berlin, Bechstein Hall, 6 November 1928
Alan Bush (piano)
Publication: Oxford University Press. Score © 1928
Manuscript: British Library, London. MS. Mus. 352, ff. 1-31: Score in ink
Bibliography: *Musical Times*, 69 (October 1928), 801 (T.A.); *The Times*,
24 June 1927, 14 (Anon.)

1927-1928

SONG TO THE MEN OF ENGLAND (Opus 10)
Partsong for unaccompanied mixed chorus (SATB)
Text: Percy Bysshe Shelley

Dedication: "For the London Labour Choral Union"

Duration: 3'
First performance: Unable to trace
Publication: J. Curwen. Vocal score © 1928 (*The Choral Handbook,
   No. 1243*)
   Republished by Joseph Williams Ltd. © 1950
Manuscript: British Library, London. MS. Mus. 422, ff. 1-11:
   Score with autograph annotations in red ink and engraver's
   annotations in pencil. Dated December 1927 - January 1928
Bibliography: *Musical Times*, 70 (January 1929), 43 (WRA)

1928

RELINQUISHMENT (Opus 11)
For piano

Dedication: "To C.K". [in the printed score only]
Duration: 8'
First performance: Berlin, Bechstein Hall, 6 November 1928
   Alan Bush (piano)
First UK performance: Unable to trace
Publication: Oxford University Press. Score © 1929
   (The piece was originally written as a contribution to a series of
   contemporary compositions edited by John Ireland for Oxford
   University Press. It was at first rejected due to its extreme difficulty,
   but published separately a few months later)
Manuscript: British Library, London. MS. Mus. 352, ff. 32-50: Score in
   ink. Dated 2 February 1928
Recordings: Redcliffe Recordings RR 008 (1994). Piers Lane (piano)
Bibliography: *Musical Times*, 70 (December 1929), 1086 (TA); *Musical
   Times*, 136 (February 1995), 108 (W. Mellers)

CRADLE SONG FOR AN UNWANTED CHILD
For voice and piano
Text: Randall Swingler

First performance: Unable to trace
Unpublished
Manuscript: British Library, London. Add. Ms. 52464B, ff. 3-7:
   Autograph fair copy

1929

DIALECTIC (Opus 15)
For string quartet

Duration: c. 15′
First performance: London, Broadcasting House, 29 March 1935
  The Brosa Quartet (Broadcast in the BBC National Programme)
Publication: Boosey & Hawkes Ltd. Score and parts © 1938 and 1947
Manuscript: Whereabouts unknown
Recordings: Claudio Records CB 5151-2 (recorded and issued in 1984;
  re-issued in 2002). The Medici String Quartet
Bibliography: *Music Teacher*, 29 (August 1950), 361+ (W.R. Anderson);
  Musical Times, 76 (October 1935), 940-42 (Anon.); *Musical
  Times*, 79 (July 1938), 536-7 (MMS); *Musical Times*,
  89 (October 1948), 303-4 (W. McNaught); *Strad*, 109
  (July 1998), 761 (R. Dunnett); *Tempo*, No. 153 (June 1985),
  39-40 (C. MacDonald); *The Times*, 30 March 1935, 16
  (Anon.); *The Times*, 2 September 1935, 8 (Anon.)
Note: This work was selected for and played at the 1935 ISCM Festival in
  Prague by the New Hungarian Quartet (*The Times*, 14/9/35, 8)

OTHER VERSIONS

Arrangement for string orchestra

First performance: London, Wigmore Hall, 30 January 1939
  The London String Orchestra, conducted by Alan Bush
Unpublished
Bibliography: *The Times*, 3 February 1939, 10 (Anon.)

1930

DANCE OVERTURE (Opus 12)
For military band

Commissioned by: The BBC

2 flutes and piccolo, 2 clarinets in Eb, 2 oboes, 3 solo clarinets in Bb, 2
ripieno clarinet in Bb, 2 2nd clarinets in Bb, 2 3rd clarinets in Bb, 1 alto
saxophone in Eb, 1 tenor saxophone in Bb, 2 bassoons, 4 horns in F, solo
and 1st cornets in Bb, 1 2nd cornet in Bb, 2 trumpets in Bb, 2 tenor

trombones, 1 bass trombone, 1 euphonium, 2 basses, 1 string bass, timpani and percussion (2 players)

Dedication: "To Edward Clark"
Duration: 14'
First performance: London, Broadcasting House, 25 April 1931
  BBC Wireless Military Band, conducted by B. Walton
  O'Donnell. Broadcast in the London National Programme
Unpublished
Manuscript: British Library, London. MS. Mus. 327 (ff. 64):
  Full score in ink. Dated September-October 1930
Recordings: To be issued in 2006. Tokyo Kosei Wind Orchestra,
  conducted by D. Bostock

OTHER VERSIONS

Arrangement for full orchestra [1935]

3.2.3+sax.2/4.3.3.1/timpani/percussion/strings

First concert performance: London, Queen's Hall, 30 August 1935
  BBC Symphony Orchestra, conducted by Alan Bush
First broadcast performance: BBC Home Service, 12 August 1953
  BBC Symphony Orchestra, conducted by John Hollingsworth
  (A broadcast from the Promenade Concerts in the Royal Albert
  Hall)
Publication: J. Williams Ltd. Full score © 1956
Manuscript: British Library, London. MS. Mus. 328 (ff. 67): Full
  score in ink
Bibliography: *Musical Times*, 94 (October 1953), 472 (D. Mitchell)

THE ROAD (Opus 13) [Also listed as Opus 13, No. 1]
Part song for unaccompanied mixed chorus (SATB)
Text: Violet H. Friedlander

Duration: 2'30"
First performance: Unable to trace
Publication: J. Curwen. Vocal score © 1930 (*The Choral Handbook,*
  No. 1255)
Manuscript: British Library, London. MS Mus. 422, ff. 12-19: Vocal
  score with autograph annotations in red ink and engraver's
  annotations in pencil with a typewritten copy of the words signed

by the author and dated 27 January 1930
Bibliography: *Musical Times*, 71 (November 1932), 992 (WRA)

SONG TO FREEDOM
For mixed chorus (SATB) and piano
Text: R.C.K. Ensor

First performance: Unable to trace
Publication: Independent Labour Party Publications Department. Vocal
  score [© 1930] in *Twelve Labour Choruses*
Manuscript: Whereabouts unknown

1931

THREE CONTRAPUNTAL STUDIES (Opus 13) [listed as Opus 13, No. 2]
For violin and viola

1.   Ground bass: Con moto moderato ma deciso [2′ 03″]
2.   Canon: Andante con moto [2′16″]
3.   Fugue: Maestoso [4′ 02″]

First performance: London, Amen House (OUP), 10 March 1933
  Members of the Chelsea String Quartet
Unpublished
Manuscript: British Library, London. MS. Mus. 352, ff. 51-75:
  Score in ink. Dated September-November 1931. Parts in ink with
  bowing marks in pencil
Recordings: Dutton CDLX 7130 (2002)
  N. Liddell (violin) and E. Turnbull (viola)
Bibliography: *The Times*, 11 March 1933, 12 (Anon.)

QUESTION AND ANSWER
Song for mixed chorus (SATB) and piano
Text: G. Roy Atterbury

First performance: Unable to trace
Publication: Workers' Music Association. Vocal score © 1931
  Reprinted 1970 in *Songs of Struggle*. Also included in
  The Left Song Book (eds. A. Bush and R. Swingler), Gollancz 1938
Manuscript: Whereabouts unknown

1932-1933

SONGS OF THE DOOMED (Opus 14)
Four songs and an Epilogue for tenor (or baritone), female chorus (SSAA)
  and piano
Texts: Frederick Cecil Boden from *Out of the Coalfields*

1. Despair is at heart and hatred for ever (Molto marcato ma non allegro)
2. When daylight's breaking (Andante penseroso)
3. Beauty dwells uncertain here in homes unsure (-)
4. Here they lie, that once had breath (-)
5. Epilogue: Hush be still you bitter thing (Andante tranquillo)(for
    chorus and piano)

Duration: 15′
First performance: London, Morley College, 8 March 1933
  Geoffrey Dunn (tenor) and the London Labour Choral Union with
  Alan Bush (piano)
Unpublished
Manuscript: British Library, London. MS. Mus 422, ff. 20-51: Vocal
  score in ink; ff. 45-48: Score of an alternative version for tenor, in
  ink, with chorus parts sketched in pencil, ff. 49-51. Dated
  February 1932-March 1933
  Another score of the third song, written a tone higher, is in Add. MS.
  52464B, ff. 1-2

1934

SONG OF THE HUNGER MARCHERS
Unison song for mixed chorus (SATB) and piano
Text: Randall Swingler

First performance: Unable to trace
Publication: *The Left Song Book* (eds. A. Bush and R. Swingler), Gollancz
  1938: Workers Music Association. Vocal score © 1950
  Also published in Moscow in 1963. Reprinted 1970 in *Songs of
  Struggle*
Manuscript: Whereabouts unknown

THE PAGEANT OF LABOUR
For mixed chorus and orchestra
A portrait of the history of the Trade Unions, Co-operative and

Labour Movements in the 18th, 19th and 20th centuries
Written by Matthew Anderson and organised by the Central Women's
  Organisation Committee to the London Trades Council
Produced by: Edward P. Genn

Musical numbers included:
Episode 1 - Capital Enslaves the Workers
  Scene 1. Domestic workers (c.1790) – Opening Chorus and Ballet
  Scene 2. The New Political Philosophy (A Room)
  Scene 3. Malthus (A Meeting Room)
  Scene 4. The Domestic Workers and the Cottage Interior – chorus,
            procession of paupers, factory bells and march out

Episode 2 - The Martyrdom of the Children (1800)
  Scene 1. The Cottage Interior
  Scene 2. The Children's Ballet
  Scene 3. Underground-Working in a Mine
  Scene 4. A Sectional view of the House of Lords, showing an
            Archbishop, Five Bishops and other members
  Scene 5. The Children's Ballet resumes

Episode 3 - Consolations of Philanthropy and Religion (1800-1820)
  in 9 scenes including Luddite Meeting, 'Pageant Song' and
  Ballet – The Triumph of the Machine

Episode 4 - London received the Chartists (1848) in 3 scenes including
  Ballroom Ballet

Episode 5 - The Triumph of the Trade Union in 4 scenes

Episode 6 - The Fletcher Family (1900-1919) in 5 scenes leading to Finale
  Ballet and 'Pageant Song'

2.1.1.0/2.1.2.1 – timpani/ percussion/strings and mixed chorus (SATB)
  (and in the ballet) 3 trumpets and 3 trombones

First performance: London, Crystal Palace, 15-20 October 1934
  Orchestra and London Labour Choral Union, conducted by Michael
  Tippett and Alan Bush

Unpublished
Manuscript: British Library, London. MS. Mus. 394-395 (2 volumes;
 ff. 71 and 44): Full score in ink with annotations in red ink and
 red crayon. Dated May-August 1934
Bibliography: The Programme Book for the *Pageant of Labour*. Copy in
 the Histon Archive; *The Times*, 16 October 1934, 16 (Anon.)

OTHER VERSIONS

Concert version of 'Men and Machines', a ballet with choral finale,
adapted and arranged from the Pageant of Labour by Alan Bush for brass,
(3 trumpets, 2 trombones), percussion, piano and chorus [1934]

Unpublished
Manuscript: British Library, London. MS. Mus. 396 (ff. 9): Score in ink

1935

PROLOGUE TO A WORKERS' MEETING (Opus 16)
For brass orchestra

Written for the International Music Bureau, Moscow

Solo cornet in Bb, soprano in Eb, ripieno and flugel-horn in Bb,
2nd and 3rd cornets in Bb, solo horn in Eb, 1st and 2nd horns in
Eb, 1st and 2nd baritones in Bb, 1st and 2nd trombones in Bb,
bass trombone, euphonium in Bb, Eb and Bb basses, drums and percussion

Duration: 7'30"
First performance: Unable to trace
Unpublished
Manuscript: Whereabouts unknown
Note: This piece was later re-written as the *Overture: Resolution*
 (Opus 25) in 1943

OTHER VERSIONS

Arrangement for brass band by the composer (1936)

Unpublished

HIS WAR OR YOURS

Ballet in three scenes with scenario by Michael Tippett

Written for the London Workers' Ballet
Instrumentation: 3 trumpets, 3 trombones, tuba and percussion
First performance: London, Co-operative House (Peckham), 28 March
  1936
  Young Workers' Ballet and the South London Brass Orchestra,
  conducted by David Ellenberg
Unpublished
Manuscript: British Library, London. MS Mus. 397 (ff. 14): Score in ink

MINING

Ballet written for the London Worker's Ballet

Instrumentation: Unable to trace
First performance: Unable to trace
  Young Workers' Ballet with ensemble, conducted by Alan Bush
Unpublished
Manuscript: Whereabouts unknown

RED FRONT

For mixed choir (SATB), speaking choir, brass (3 trumpets, 3 trombones
and tuba) and percussion
Text: Sylvia Townsend Warner

Duration: c. 5'
First performance: London, Co-operative House (Peckham), 28 March
  1936
  The London Labour Choral Union and the South London Brass
  Orchestra, conducted by Alan Bush
Unpublished
Manuscript: Whereabouts unknown

1936

CONCERT-PIECE (Opus 17)

For cello and piano

Duration: c. 20'
First performances: Prague, 27 and 29 November 1936. Juliette Alvin
  (cello) and Alan Bush (piano)

First British performance: London, Mercury Theatre, 11 January 1937
  Norina Semino (cello) and Alan Bush (piano) (An Iris Lemare
  Concert)
First broadcast performance: London, Broadcasting House, 12 March
  1937 in the BBC National Programme
  Juliette Alvin (cello) and Alan Bush (piano)
Publication: Maecenas Music. Score © 2004. Published in association
  with the Alan Bush Music Trust
Manuscript: British Library, London. MS. Mus. 352 (ff. 76-127): Score in
  ink. Dated May-September 1936
  Cello part also in ink. Written substantially later (*circa* 1980)
Recordings: Meridian Records CDE 84458 (2002). Joseph Spooner
  (cello) and Catherine Summerhayes (piano)
Bibliography: *Musical Times*, 78 (February 1937), 166-7 (MMS);
  Musical Times, 78 (April 1937), 365 (MMS): *Musical Times*, 78
  (July 1937), 650 (I. Schwerke); *The Times*, 18 January 1937, 8
  (Anon.); *The Times*, 22 June 1937, 14 (Anon.)
Note: This work was selected for and played at the 1937 ISCM Festival in
  Paris on 21 June 1937 by V. Palotai (cello) and Alan Bush (piano)

LABOUR'S SONG OF CHALLENGE
For mixed chorus (SATB), unison chorus and piano
Text: Randall Swingler

Duration: 5'
First performance: Unable to trace
Publication: London Labour Choral Union. Vocal score © 1936
Manuscript: Whereabouts unknown

THEME
For organ
One of four themes submitted to André Marchal (blind organist of St.
Germain-des-Près in Paris) for the improvisation of a four movement work
in the form of a symphony. Besides Alan Bush composing the subject for a
Fugue, William Walton contributed the theme for an *Adagio*, Benjamin
Britten for a *Scherzo* and Constant Lambert for a *Toccata*

Commissioned by: Felix Aprahamian as secretary of The Organ
  Music Society
First performance: London, St. John's Church, Red Lion Square, 12
  November 1936. André Marchal (organ)
Manuscript: Whereabouts unknown

Publication: The themes were printed for the Society by Boosey & Hawkes
Bibliography: *Musical Times*, 77 (December 1936), 1104+1111-1113
  (Alan Frank)
Note: This was the second of such concerts organised by the Organ Music
  Society, the first being given a year earlier on 10 December 1935
  when Marchal first played in London.
  On that occasion, Roussel provided the subjects for the *Prelude* to
  the four-movement work and the *Fugue*, Sibelius contributed the
  theme for an *Adagio*, Jongen contributed the theme for the
  Scherzo and Vaughan Williams the theme for a *Toccata*

1936-1937

CONCERTO FOR PIANO AND ORCHESTRA (Opus 18)
in four movements

1. Con moto moderato ma deciso
2. Con vivicato, ma non troppo allegro
3. Grave
4. Allegro vigoroso ma non troppo

The last movement includes a setting of words by Randall Swingler for
  baritone solo and male chorus (TTBB)

3.3.3.3/4.3.3.1/timpani/percussion/harp/strings

Dedication: "To Nancy Bush"
Duration: 57'
First performance: London, BBC Broadcasting House, 4 March 1938
  Alan Bush (piano), Dennis Noble (baritone), the BBC Male Voice
  Chorus, and the BBC Symphony Orchestra, conducted by Adrian
  Boult
First concert performance (Lento and Finale only): London, Queen's
  Hall, 5 April 1939 (during the Festival of Music for the People)
  Alan Bush (piano), Dennis Noble (baritone), the Co-operative and
  Labour Choirs, and the London Symphony Orchestra, conducted
  by Constant Lambert
First complete concert performance: London, Northern Polytechnic
  (Holloway), 15 May 1954
  Margaret Kitchin (piano), John Hargreaves (baritone), the Male
  Voice Choir and the Modern Symphony Orchestra, conducted by
  Arthur Dennington

Publication: Alan Bush. Full score © 1956 (reproduced from the autograph)
Manuscript: British Library, London. MS. Mus. 329-331: 3 volumes. Full
score in ink. Dated 22 December 1937
Bibliography: *BMS Newsletter*, No. 79 (September 1998), 205-7
(P. Conway); *The Listener*, 19, No. 476 (23 February 1938), 437
(S. Goddard); *Musical Times*, 79 (April 1938), 295-6 (F); *Musical
Times*, 95 (July 1954), 382 (Anon.); *Strad*, 65 (May 1954), 5
(Anon.); *The Times*, 7 March 1938, 12 (Anon.)

OTHER VERSIONS

Arrangement for two pianos
by the composer

Publication: Joseph Williams Ltd. Score © 1938
Manuscript: British Library, London. MS. Mus. 331. Score, in ink, with
occasional performance annotations in pencil. The final page of
the third movement and the parts of the start of the fourth have new
pages, perhaps written circa 1980, pasted over the score. With a
score of the baritone solo part, accompanied by a reduction of the
piano and orchestral parts for piano solo (ff. 98-104)

1938

PAGEANT OF CO-OPERATION (Alternative title: Towards Tomorrow)
For military band and mixed chorus
Scenario by: Montagu Slater and André van Gyseghem
Dances arranged by: Margaret Barr, Katie Eisenstaedt and Teda de Mor

Musical numbers included:
Episode 1. Fanfares, Chorus: 'The Lonely Plough'
            Morris Dance – Sound of the Sirens

Episode 2. Procession and rhythm of the Machines
            Solo leading to chorus: 'Men of England'

Episode 3. Robert Owen's speech; Children's Tableaux

Episode 4. The Rochdale Pioneers leading to

Episode 5. Procession showing the growth of the Co-operative
            Movement

Episode 6.   War is declared – bugles, artillery fire, leading to
            Attack and War Ballet

Episode 7.   Ballet of mourning women; Chorus: 'We are Women'

Episode 8.   International Procession – Ballet of Young Workers leading to
            Tableaux of national costumes; Fanfare leading to 'Men Awake'

2.2.3.1/2.3 (+ 4 cornets). 3.1/timpani/percussion and double bass

First performance: London, Wembley Stadium, 2 July 1938
  Members of the London/South Suburban/Watford Co-operative
  Societies (with speaking parts and ensemble), directed by Alan
  Bush
Unpublished
Manuscript: British Library, London. MS. Mus. 398-399: Full score in
  pencil (MS. Mus. 398, 5 and 6, together with 399, 1-10 in ink);
  MS. Mus. 400-403: parts in ink
MS Mus. 398 includes:
  ff. 3-4 'Bonny Green Garters', arranged by Bush
  ff. 5-8 'The Beaux of the City of London', arranged by Bush
  ff. 9-13 'Lucky Locket' and 'Tom, Tom, the Piper's Son', arranged
  by Alan Bush
  ff. 14-16 'Come Lasses and Lads', arranged by Bush
  ff. 17-44 'Machine Ballet'
  ff. 45-58 'Men of England'
  ff. 59-60 'The Mulberry Bush', arranged by Bush
  ff. 61-87 'Pigeon Music': a medley comprising arrangements of
  'England, Arise!', 'God Save the People', Workers' March
  ['John Brown's Body'], 'Cwm Rhondda' and 'Rebel Song'
MS Mus. 399 includes:
  ff. 1-33 'War Ballet'
  ff. 34-37 'The Red Flag'. Two arrangements
  ff. 38-39 'Scots, Wha Hae', arranged by Bush
  ff. 40-43 'Men of Harlech', arranged by Bush
  ff. 44-45 'The Wearing of the Green', arranged by Bush
  ff. 46-49 'The Marseillaise', arranged by Bush
  ff. 50-53 'Czechoslovak National Anthem', arranged by Bush
  ff. 54-55 Yankee Yoodle [*sic*], arranged by Bush
  ff. 56-57 'Way Down Upon the Swanee River', arranged by Bush
  ff. 58-61 'Austrian Workers' Song', arranged by Bush

ff. 62-66 'Young Comrades' Song (Jazz Comedy)', arranged by
Alan Bush
Bibliography: *The Times*, 4 July 1938, 20 (Anon.)

1939

THE PRISON CYCLE [PAGES FROM 'THE SWALLOW BOOK']
(Opus 19). Written in collaboration with Alan Rawsthorne
For mezzo-soprano and piano
Text: Ernst Toller from *Schwalbenbuch*

1. Introduction: Sechs Schritte her, sechs Schritte hin, Ohne Sinn
    (AB)(Andante lentamente)
2. Song: Die Dinge, die erst Feindlich zu dir Schauen (AB) (Andantino
    piacevole)

3. Interlude: Sechs Schritte her, sechs Schritte hin, Ohne Sinn (AR)
    (Poco gravamente)
4. Song: Über mir aug dem Holzrahmen des halbgeoeffneten
    Gitterfensters (AR) (Andante)

5. Epilogue: Sechs Schritte her, sechs Schritte hin, Ohne Sinn (AB)
    (Grave)

Duration: 10′
First (private) performance: London, Duke's Hall (Royal Academy of
  Music), 12 October 1939
  Anne Wood (mezzo-soprano) and Alan Bush (piano)
First public performance: London, Conway Hall, 15 December 1939
  Anne Wood (mezzo-soprano) and Alan Bush (piano)
Publication: Forsyth Brothers Ltd. (Manchester). Vocal score © 2001
Manuscript: RAM, London: Nos.1, 2 and 5 (MS Lam 502)
  RNCM, Manchester: Nos. 3 and 4 (RNCM ms.026)
Recordings: Campion Records Cameo 2021 (2003). Alison Wells
  (soprano) and Keith Swallow (piano)
Bibliography: *Clarion*, 8 (2005-6), 3 (M. Jones)

OTHER VERSIONS

Arrangement for baritone and piano

First performance: London, Purcell Room, 24 October 1977
  Graham Titus (baritone) and Eric Levi (piano)
First broadcast performance: BBC Radio 3, 28 February 1978
  Graham Titus (baritone) and Alan Bush (piano)

MAKE YOUR MEANING CLEAR

Unison song for mixed chorus and piano
Text: Randall Swingler

Duration: 3′
First performance: London, Conway Hall, 15 December 1939
  Combined WMA choirs with Alan Bush (piano)
Publication: Workers Music Association. Vocal score © 1939
  Reprinted 1970 in *Songs of Struggle*. Also included in
  a collection of *Peace Songs*, edited by John Jordan
  Kahn & Averill for the WMA © 1989
Manuscript: Whereabouts unknown. Sketches in BL Deposit 2005/32

FESTIVAL OF MUSIC FOR THE PEOPLE

Music for a pageant in 10 episodes to a scenario by Randall
Swingler

Music specially composed and arranged in ten episodes as follows:

PART 1

Flourish for Wind Band   (Ralph Vaughan Williams)
Introduction   (Arnold Cooke)
Episode 1: Feudal England   (Elisabeth Lutyens)
Episode 2: The Massacre of the Innocents   (Victor Yates – Basque
              Lullaby arr. Edmund Rubbra)
Episode 3: Peasants in Revolt   (Erik Chisholm)
Episode 4: Soldiers of Freedom   (Christian Darnton)
Episode 5: Village Green to Concert Hall   (Frederic Austin)

PART 2

Episode 6: Changing Europe   (Norman Demuth)
Episode 7: Prisoners   (Alan Bush)
Episode 8: Slaves   (featuring Paul Robeson and a Negro Choir)

First performance: Unable to trace
Publication: Workers' Music Association. Vocal score © 1940
  No. 4 published separately 1951
  No. 5 published separately 1947 (also arranged for 2-part
  women's voices (SA). Reprinted 1970 in *Songs of Struggle*
  No. 6 published separately 1951 (as *Truth on the March*)
  Reprinted 1970 in *Songs of Struggle*. Also included in a
  collection of *Peace Songs* edited by John Jordan
  Kahn & Averill for the WMA © 1989
Manuscript: British Library, London. MS. Mus. 407,ff. 1-19:
  Score in ink

THE STAR TURNS RED
Incidental music to the play (in four acts) by Sean O'Casey
Produced by John Allen

Music written for the following:

Introduction to Act I (Moderato)
End of Act 1
Introduction to Act II (Con moto)
End of Act II

Introduction to Act III
End of Act III
Introduction to Act IV
End of Act IV

Instrumentation: 3 trumpets, percussion (2), violin and piano
First performance: London, Unity Theatre, 12 March 1940
  Unable to trace the players. Conducted by Alan Bush and David
  Ellenberg (The music was pre-recorded onto 78 rpm discs)
Unpublished. The play was published by Macmillan & Co. in 1940
Manuscript: British Library, London. MS. Mus. 406 (ff. 11): Score in ink,
  with annotations in red ink and pencil
Bibliography: *The Times*, 14 March 1940, 6 (Anon.)

1941

MARCH OF THE WORKERS
For mixed chorus (SATB) and piano

Text: William Morris

Duration: 3'
First performance: Unable to trace
Publication: Workers' Music Association. Vocal score © 1950
Manuscript: Unable to trace. Sketches in BL deposit 2005/32

OTHER VERSIONS

Arrangement for unison chorus and orchestra
by Alan Bush for the WMA Summer School, Wortley Hall, August 1963

1+recorder.1+3.2 sax/2.3.0.0/2 guitars/accordian/piano/percussion/strings

Unpublished
Manuscript: British Library, London. MS. Mus. 418, ff. 106-112: Full score
  in ink

UNITE AND BE FREE: For the Peoples of India and Britain
Unison song for mixed voices (SATB) and piano
Text: Alan Bush

Duration: 4'
First performance: Unable to trace
Publication: Workers' Music Association. Vocal score © 1941
Manuscript: Whereabouts unknown

THE GREAT RED ARMY
Song for mixed chorus (SATB) (or 2-part female voices (SSAA))
and piano
Text: Randall Swingler

First performance: included in a broadcast of 'British Songs' on the BBC
  American and Empire Service, 23 August 1942
  Unable to trace the performers
Publication: Workers' Music Association. Vocal score © 1942
  Reprinted 1970 in *Songs of Struggle*
Manuscript: Whereabouts unknown. Sketch in BL Deposit 2005/32

MEDITATION ON A GERMAN SONG OF 1848 (Opus 22)
For solo violin and piano or string orchestra

Duration: 9′
First performance: Cambridge, Arts Theatre, 9 November 1941
  Max Rostal (violin) and the London String Orchestra,
  conducted by Alan Bush
First London performance: Aeolian Hall, 6 December 1941
  Max Rostal (violin) and the London String Orchestra,
  conducted by Alan Bush
Publication: Joseph Williams Ltd. Full score © 1948
  Violin part edited by Max Rostal
Manuscript: British Library, London. MS. Mus. 334 (ff. ii + 8):
  Full score in ink
Note: The song is *Reiterlied* or *The Trooper's Pledge* with words by
  Georg Herwegh, translated by Nancy Bush

OTHER VERSIONS

Arrangement for violin and piano
by the composer

First performance: London, Contemporary Music Centre, 15 May 1944
  Max Rostal (violin) and Alan Bush (piano)
Publication: Joseph Williams Ltd. Score © 1948. Violin part edited by
  Max Rostal
Recordings: Meridian Records CDE 8441 (© 20040. Adam Summerhayes
  (violin) and Katherine Summerhayes (piano)

1942

FESTAL DAY (Opus 23)
Overture for orchestra
Composed as a tribute to Ralph Vaughan Williams on his 70th birthday
(Original title was 'Birthday Greeting in Honour of Vaughan Williams';
also entitled 'Birthday Overture' on the composer's recording of the work)

Commissioned by: The BBC

1.1.2.2/2.2.1.0/percussion/piano/strings

Duration: 4′10″
First performance: Bedford, Corn Exchange, 12 October 1942
  Section of the London Symphony Orchestra, conducted by
  Clarence Raybould (Broadcast on the BBC Home Service at

6.45pm, the first of six special programmes, introduced by Hubert
Foss, in celebration of Vaughan Williams's 70th birthday)
Unpublished
Manuscript: British Library, London. MS. Mus. 335, ff. 1-18: Full score in
ink
Bibliography: *Musical Times*, 83 (October 1942), 334-5 (WRA)
Note: In a letter, dated 28 September 1942, to L .A. Duncan at the BBC,
the composer revealed that the work "… contains a passing
quotation from a fanfare which Dr Vaughan Williams wrote
specially as the opening to the "Festival of Music for the People",
held in 1935…. It is intended as a token of gratitude and esteem
from a younger fighter in the cause of freedom and progress to a
veteran campaigner in the same field."

THE DUKE IN DARKNESS
Incidental music for chamber orchestra to the play (in three acts) by
Patrick Hamilton
Produced by Michael Redgrave

1.1.1.1/1.0.1.0/percussion and strings

Duration of the music: 23′
First performance: London, Aldwych Theatre, 8 October 1942
  Music played by 26 session musicians, conducted by Alan Bush
  This music was pre-recorded by Levi's Sound Studios Ltd under
  the composer's direction
  Cast included Michael Redgrave, Leslie Banks and Hugh Burden
Unpublished. The play was published by Constable in 1943
Manuscript: British Library, London. MS. Mus. 407, ff. 20-51: Score
in ink.
Bibliography: Strachen, A. *Secret Dreams: The Biography of Michael
Redgrave*. London, Weidenfeld & Nicolson, 2004, 206-211;
The Times, 9 October 1942, 6 (Anon.)
Note: After its London run, the play was taken on tour to Edinburgh (The
Lyceum), Newcastle-upon-Tyne (Theatre Royal), and Leeds
(Grand Theatre) and then returned to London at St. James's Theatre

RUSSIAN GLORY – MILITARY MARCH ON SOVIET SONGS (Opus 20)
For military band
Based on *Song of the Fatherland* (Isaac Dunayevsky) and the Trio from
Song of Stalin (Aram Khachaturian)

Commissioned by the BBC for use by the BBC Military Band in Overseas
  Programmes

2 flutes and piccolo, 2 clarinets in Eb, 2 oboes , 3 solo clarinets in Bb, 2
ripieno clarinet in Bb, 2 2nd clarinet in Bb, 2 3rd clarinet in Bb, 1 alto
saxophone in Eb, 1 tenor saxophone in Bb, 2 bassoons, 4 horns in F, solo
and 1st cornets in Bb, 1 2nd cornet in Bb, 2 trumpets in Bb, 2 tenor
trombones, 1 bass trombone, 1 euphonium, 2 basses, 1 string bass, timpani
and percussion (2 players)

Dedication: According to a BBC memo (dated 7 September 1944), the
  dedication appeared on the cover thus: "Dedicated to the soldiers
  of the Red Army, and with grateful acknowledgement to my good
  friend, Corporal Sydney Latuski and Private Albert Harris of the
  British Forces, whose thorough knowledge of the Military March
  has been of great help to me in working this out."
Duration: 6′
First performance: Recorded by the BBC Military Band on 15 March 1943
  (recording No. 11615/6)
Unpublished
Manuscript: Whereabouts unknown

FANTASIA ON SOVIET THEMES
For military band and containing:

(1) Partisan Song: A revolutionary folk-song of the wars of 1919-21 (-)
(2) Collective Farm Song of 1931-35 (Allegro vivace)
(3) Cheerful Song for Solo and Chorus by Zacharov (Allegro grazioso)
(4) Death of Chapayev-funeral march for a partisan leader by Sedoi (-)
(5) Molodezhnaya [Song of Youth] for Childrens' Choir by Isaac
     Dunayevsky (Allegro vivace)
(6) Finale

Commissioned by the BBC for the BBC Military Band

2 flutes and piccolo, 2 clarinets in Eb, 2 oboes, 3 solo clarinets in Bb, 2
ripieno clarinet in Bb, 2 2nd clarinets in Bb, 2 3rd clarinets in Bb, 1 alto
saxophone in Eb, 1 tenor saxophone in Bb, 2 bassoons, 4 horns in F, solo
and 1st cornet in Bb, 1 2nd cornet in Bb, 2 trumpets in Bb, 2 tenor
trombones, 1 bass trombone, 1 euphonium, 2 basses, 1 string bass, timpani
and percussion (2 players)

"Dedicated in affectionate homage to Madame Agnes Maisky [wife of the
  Soviet Ambassador] for so long the gracious representative of the
  Soviet People, as a humble tribute to whom this work is designed"
Duration: 10′
First performance: Recorded by the BBC Military Band on 15 March 1943
  (recording No. 11610/2)
Unpublished
Manuscript: Whereabouts unknown

OTHER VERSIONS

FANTASIA ON SOVIET THEMES (Opus 24)
Arranged for full orchestra (1944)

The same Soviet themes were used except the Finale was replaced by an
Introduction (Allegro maestoso)

Commissioned by the BBC for the 51st Season of Henry Wood Promenade
Concerts

2+1.2.2.2/4.2.3.1/timpani/ percussion/glockenspiel/strings

Dedication: As above
Duration: 11′
First performance: London, Royal Albert Hall, 27 July 1945
  London Symphony Orchestra, conducted by Alan Bush
Publication: Novello & Co. Ltd. Full score © 1944
Manuscript: British Library, London. MS. Mus. 335, ff. 19-69: Full score
  in black and blue ink
Bibliography: A. Bush: *Programmes notes* for the first performance;
  Musical Times, 86 (September 1945), 285 (F. Bonavia); *The
  Times*, 28 July 1945, 6 (Anon.)

BRITAIN'S PART
Song for speaker, mixed chorus (SATB), percussion and piano
Text: Alan Bush

Duration: 8′
First performance: London, Conway Hall, 24 October 1942
  WMA Chorus and Alan Bush (piano), conducted by David
  Ellenberg

Publication: WMA Chorus parts only © 1942
Manuscript: British Library, London. MS. Mus. 416, ff. 36-50

1943

TOULON
Song for mezzo-soprano, mixed chorus (SATB) and piano
Text: Nancy Bush

Commissioned by: The Birmingham Anglo-Soviet Unity Group
Duration: 4′
First performance: Birmingham, Midland Institute, 26 May 1943
  The Birmingham Clarion Singers and Lillian Green's Mixed
  Choir (A WMA concert for the Birmingham Anglo-Soviet
  Unity Group)
First London performance: Queen Mary Hall, 6 January 1945
  Jane Charlton (mezzo-soprano), WMA Singers, Muriel
  Rubens (piano), conducted by Alan Bush
Unpublished
Manuscript: British Library, London. MS. Mus. 422, ff. 52-55; score in
  pencil: Deposit 2005/32

FREEDOM ON THE MARCH
Song for solo, mixed chorus and symphony orchestra
Text: Randall Swingler
Written to mark the 2nd anniversary of the Nazi invasion of the USSR

First performance: London, Royal Albert Hall, 27 June 1943
  Combined choirs and London Philharmonic Orchestra, conducted
  by Alan Bush
  (The British-Soviet Unity Demonstration)
Unpublished
Manuscript: Whereabouts unknown
Bibliography: *The Times*, 28 June 1943, 2 (Anon.)
Note: From a letter which Bush sent to the Performing Right Society
  (dated 7 July 1943), it is evident that he also contributed two
  fanfares [for brass] to the programme

RESOLUTION (Opus 25) [originally numbered Opus 24]
Overture for orchestra [Originally Opus 24, later corrected to Opus 25]

2.2.2.2/4.2.3.0/timpani/percussion/piano/strings

Duration: 7'
First performance: Bedford, Corn Exchange, 1 February 1944
  BBC Orchestra (Section B), conducted by Clarence Raybould
  (Broadcast by the BBC on the Home Service)
Publication: Joseph Williams Ltd. Full score © 1947
Manuscript: British Library, London. MS. Mus. 336 (ff. iii + 21): Bound
  full score in ink with conductor's markings in blue crayon and
  pencil. Dated 29 August 1943
Note: This work is based on *Prologue for a Workers Meeting* for
  Brass Band Opus 16 (1935)

OTHER VERSIONS

Arrangement for solo piano
by the composer

Publication: J. Williams Ltd. © 1947
Manuscript: British Library, London. MS. Mus. 335, ff. 70-76: Score in
  ink and transposed down a major 3rd

1944

LYRIC INTERLUDE (Opus 26)
For solo violin with piano accompaniment

1.   Moderato ma sempre con anima
2.   Andantino
3.   Allegretto vivace
4.   Come primo
5.   Allegretto vivace

Dedication: "To Nancy Bush"
Duration: 15'30"
First performance: London, Queen Mary Hall, 6 January 1945
  Max Rostal (violin) and Alan Bush (piano)
First broadcast performance: BBC Third Programme, 2 June 1960
  Ralph Holmes (violin) and Alan Bush (piano)
Publication: Joseph Williams Ltd. Score © 1947 (Violin part edited by
  Max Rostal who also "suggested many passages")
Manuscript: British Library, London MS. Mus. 353, ff. 1-22: Score in ink
  with annotations in pencil. Dated September - October 1944
Recordings: Meridian Records CDE 84481 (© 2004)

Adam Summerhayes (violin) and Catherine Summerhayes (piano)
Bibliography: *Musical Times*, 89 (March 1948), 85 (F. Bonavia); *Musical
Times*, 136 (February 1995), 108 (W. Mellers); *The Times*, 8
January 1945, 8 (Anon.)

SONG TO THE COMMONS OF ENGLAND
For unison or mixed voices (SATB) and piano
Text: Miles Carpenter

Duration: 3′
First performance: London, Queen Mary Hall, 6 January 1945
  WMA Singers with Muriel Rubens (piano), conducted by
  Alan Bush
Publication: Workers' Music Association. Vocal score © 1944
  Also published in Moscow in 1963 (for baritone solo only)
Manuscript: British Library, London. MS. Mus. 422, ff. 56-58

ESQUISSE: LE QUARTORZE JUILLET (Opus 38)
For piano
Written in commemoration of the French resistance movement – the
piece makes use of two famous songs of the Revolution: 'La Carmagnole'
and 'Ça ira'

Originally commissioned by Felix Aprahamian for a *Free French
  Piano Album* in 1944
Duration: 3′15″
First performance: London, Broadcasting House, 29 May 1947
  Kyla Greenbaum (piano) (Broadcast in the BBC Third
  Programme)
First (public) performance: London, Academy Hall (Institute of
  Contemporary Arts), 17 February 1948
  Kyla Greenbaum (piano)
Publication: Joseph Williams Ltd. Score © 1953
Manuscript: Whereabouts unknown. Sketches in BL Deposit 2005/32
Recordings: Meridian Records CDE 84481 (© 2004). Catherine
  Summerhayes (piano)
Bibliography: *Music and Letters*, 34 (July 1953), 268 (Anon.); *Music
  Review*, 15 (May 1954), 153 (Anon.); *Musical Opinion*, 76
  (March 1953), 351

1945-1946

ENGLISH SUITE (Opus 28)
For string orchestra
In three movements

(1) Fantasia (Andante con moto): on a re-composed version of the Gregorian melody used by the 17th century English composers in their 'In Nomines'
(2) Soliloquy on a Sailor's Song (Andante tranquillo): Based on a shanty 'Lowlands my Lowlands'
(3) Introduction (Allegro) and Passacaglia on 'The Cutty Wren' (a tempo piu tranquillo): Based on an English peasant song from the war of 1381

Duration: 22'
First performance: London, Wigmore Hall, 9 February 1946
  The London String Orchestra conducted by Alan Bush
First broadcast performance: London, Broadcasting House, 9 May 1946
  The London String Orchestra, conducted by Alan Bush
  (Broadcast in the BBC Home Service)
Publication: Joseph Williams Ltd. Full score © 1950
Manuscript: Whereabouts unknown
Bibliography: *Canon*, 3 (June 1950), 665 (Anon.); *The Chesterian*, 25 (July 1950), 22 (Anon.); *Monthly Musical Record*, 80 (September 1959), 189 (Anon.); *Music and Letters*, 31 (October 1950), 374-75 (Anon.); *Music Review*, 11 (November 1950), 334-35 (Anon.); *Music Survey*, 3 (March 1951), 184 (Anon.); *Musical Quarterly* 37 (April 1951), 266 (W. Mellers); *Musical Times*, 86 (April 1945), 123 (Anon.); *Musical Times*, 136 (February 1995), 108 (W. Mellers); *Strad*, 61 (July 1950), 100 (Anon.); *The Times*, 12 February 1946, 8 (Anon.)

OTHER VERSIONS

The Cutty Wren
Arranged for brass band by the composer

First performance: Unable to trace
Unpublished
Manuscript: Whereabouts unknown. Copy in the Histon archive

1946

THE PRESS GANG (or 'THE ESCAP'D APPRENTICE')
Children's operetta in three scenes with libretto by Nancy Bush
The adventures of William, a shoemaker's apprentice in the days of
  sailing ships and press gangs, who is forced to join a man-of-
  war against his will

Principals: William, a shoemaker's apprentice; Lucy, the shoemaker's
  daughter, his true love; Sarah, his deserted sweetheart;
  Captain Rapscallion, leader of the Press Gang; Mahogany Joe, an
  old sailor
Chorus of Fishermen, Fishergirls, Sailors, Members of the Press Gang and
  Sailors
Time: The second half of the eighteenth century
Scene 1: The quay of Falmouth Town
Scene 2: The hold of HMS 'Dreadnought' at anchor in the bay
Scene 3: The living-room of the shoemaker's house in Falmouth

Duration: 60'
First performance: Letchworth, St. Christopher School, 7 March
  1947. Pupils of St. Christopher School with Ursula Clutterbuck
  (piano). Produced by Reginald Snell
First London performance: Rudolf Steiner Hall, 26 April 1948
  Unable to trace details of the performers
First broadcast performance: BBC Television, Alexander Palace, 28
  December 1949. Junior members of Watford Co-operative Society.
  Music direction by Gladys Ritchie and conducted by Alan Bush.
  Stage production by George Fisher
Publication: MitteldeutscherVerlag, Halle
  Vocal score © 1953
Manuscript: Whereabouts unknown
Bibliography: *Musical Times*, 88 (March 1947), 95-96

JOSEPH'S NARRATION
Song for baritone and piano
Text: Randall Swingler

First performance: Unable to trace. The song was sung at the
  composer's 75th birthday concert on 11 January 1976 at the
  Wigmore Hall by Graham Titus (baritone) and Alan Bush (piano)
Unpublished

Manuscript: Whereabouts unknown
Bibliography: *The Times*, 12 January 1976, 15 (J. Chissell)

THE LIVING ENGLISH
A Song Pageant of People based on English Folk Songs selected by
A.L. Lloyd and arranged by Alan Bush
Script by Maurice Carpenter and produced by F.G. Lloyd

Music arranged by Alan Bush for flute, oboe, clarinet, harp,
  violin, viola, cello, narrator, mezzo-soprano and baritone soloists,
  mixed chorus (SATB) and children's chorus

PART I

Sheep-Shearing (Full Chorus)
Geordie (Men and Women)
High Germany (Women)
Lowlands, My Lowlands (Men and Women)
High Barbary (Men and Women)
A Seaman's Life (Men and Women)
Michaelmas Morn (Children)

PART II

The Water is Wide (Men and Women)
Elsie Marley (Women)
Hares on the Mountains (Men and Women)
Turtle Dove (Men and Women)
Time for us to Leave Her (Men)
Collier's Rant (Men and Women)
Bonny at Morn (Women)

FINALE

Morning Comes Early (Full Chorus)

First performance: London, Scala Theatre, 26 October 1946 as part of the
  Folk Song and Dance Festival
  Massed choirs of the London Co-operative Society Ltd. And Orchestra,
  conducted by Alan Bush
  Ballad Singer: Richard Wood
  Soloist: Margaret Eaves

Narrator: Margaret Arnott
Violinist: Elsie Avril

Unpublished except those titles above in italics. See arrangements of works
  by other composers for more details
Manuscript: British Library, London. MS. Mus. 408 (ff. 73) and 409
  (i + 87)
  Drafts and preparatory material, in pencil and ink, together
  with scripts, vocal and full scores in ink

OTHER VERSIONS

Four Faces of a People
Ten English folksongs selected with commentary by A.L. Lloyd and
arranged by Alan Bush

First performance: London, Conway Hall, 22 March 1948
  Radlett Singers and WMA Singers, conducted by Alan Bush
Bibliography: *Musical Times*, 89 (May 1948), 157 (Anon.)
Unpublished

A WORLD FOR LIVING
Unison song for mixed chorus (SATB) and piano
Text: Randall Swingler

First performance: London, Conway Hall, 22 March 1948
  WMA Singers with Gwendoline Mullins (piano),
  conducted by Alan Bush
Publication: WMA Vocal score © 1948
Manuscript: Whereabouts unknown

HOMAGE TO WILLIAM STERNDALE BENNETT (Opus 27)
For string orchestra (based on his *Piano Sonata* (Opus 46),
'The Maid of Orleans', written in 1873, two years before
Sterndale Bennett's death)

Duration: 8′
First performance: London, Wigmore Hall, 9 February 1946
  The London String Orchestra, conducted by Alan Bush
First broadcast performance: BBC Light Programme, 1 August 1946
  The London String Orchestra, conducted by Alan Bush

Unpublished
Manuscript: British Library, London. MS. Mus.335, ff. 77-82: Full
  score in ink; sketches in Deposit 2005/32
Bibliography: *Musical Times*, 86 (April 1945), 123 (Anon.); *The
  Times*, 12 February 1946, 8 (Anon.)

THE WINTER JOURNEY (Opus 29)
A cantata for soprano and baritone soli, mixed chorus (SATB) with
accompaniment for string quartet and harp or piano
Text: Randall Swingler

Introduction (Adagio)
(1) The City (Allegro)
(2) The Journey (A tempo un poco largamente)
(3) The Sleepers in the City (Andante con moto)
(4) Mary's Song (Andante con moto)
(5) Finale Chorale (Andante serioso)

Duration: 22′30″
First performance: Alnwick, Parish Church of St. Michael and All
  Angels, 14 December 1946
  Elly Short (soprano), Robert Pagan (baritone), Alnwick
  Parish Church Choir, Glaston and District Choral Society and
  Alnwick Ladies Choir with Maria Korchinska (harp) and
  Quintet (leader: Cyril Perfect), conducted by Alan Bush
  (Broadcast by the BBC in the Third Programme)
First London performance: Winchmore Hill Congregational Church
  (Compton Road, N. 21), 22 December 1946
  The WMA Choir, conducted by Alan Bush
  Unable to trace the soloists. In a BBC memo from Herbert
  Murrill to the Deputy Director of Music (dated 19 October 1946),
  it is stated that 'The soloists are not yet fixed'.
Publication: Joseph Williams Ltd. Vocal score © 1947
Manuscript: British Library, London. MS. Mus. 416, ff. 51-76 (vocal and
  piano score); sketches in Deposit 2005/32
Bibliography: *American Choral Review*, 9 No. 3 (1967), 30 (J. Grigsby)
  Musical Times, 89 (May 1948), 157 (Anon.); *Musical Times*,
  93 (February 1952), 75-76 (W.R. Anderson); *Musical Times*,
  94 (February 1953), 82 (Anon.); *Musical Times*, 109 (February 1968),
  154 (R. Crichton)

1946-1947

PIERS PLOWMAN'S DAY (Opus 30)
Symphonic Suite for orchestra

The Keep (Allegro)
The Bower (Andante con moto)
The Forest (Grave)

2.2.2.2/4.2.3.0/timpani/percussion/strings
Duration: 26'
First performance: Prague, Radio Headquarters, October 1947
  Prague Radio Orchestra, conducted by Alan Bush
First British performance: London, Royal Albert Hall, 7 September 1951
  BBC Symphony Orchestra, conducted by Alan Bush
Publication: Joseph Williams Ltd. Full score © 1956
Manuscript: British Library, London. MS. Mus. 337 (ff. iii + 83): Bound
  full score in ink, with conductor's annotations in blue pencil, red
  ink and pencil
Bibliography: *Music Review*, 12 (November 1951), 309-310 (Anon.);
  Musical Times, 92 (October 1951), 470-71 (W. Mann); *The Times*,
  8 September 1951, 8 (Anon.)

1946-1948

CONCERTO FOR VIOLIN AND ORCHESTRA (Opus 32)
In three movements

(1) Allegro deciso
(2) Andante espressivo
(3) Allegro vivace

2.2.2.2/4.3.3+1.0/timpani/percussion/strings

Dedication: "To Max Rostal as a grateful tribute to his artistry as a
  violinist and encouragement as a friend"
Duration: 26'
First performance: London, Royal Albert Hall, 25 August 1949
  Max Rostal (violin) and the London Philharmonic Orchestra,
  conducted by Basil Cameron
First broadcast performance: BBC Third Programme, 25 August 1949
  Relay from the Royal Albert Hall of the above performance

Publication: Joseph Williams Ltd. Full score © 1948
Manuscript: British Library, London. MS. Mus. 338 (ff. 177): Full
  score in black and blue ink; sketches in Deposit 2005/32
Recordings: Claudio Records CB5151-2 (recorded and issued in 1984,
  re-issued in 2002). Manoug Parikian (violin) with the BBC
  Symphony Orchestra, conducted by Norman del Mar
Bibliography: *Musical Times*, 90 (October 1949), 365-66 (W. Mann);
  Musical Times, 93 (September 1952), 408-409 (W.R. Anderson);
  Strad, 62 (July 1951), 84+86 (N.G. Long); *Tempo*, No. 153
  (June 1985), 39-40 (C. MacDonald); *The Times*, 29 August
  1949, 8 (Anon.)

OTHER VERSIONS

Arrangement for violin and piano
by the composer

Publication: Joseph Williams Ltd. Score and part © 1951. Edited by
  Max Rostal
Manuscript: British Library, London. MS. Mus. 339 (ff. 49): Score in ink,
  with engraver's markings in pencil
Bibliography: *Music Review*, 13 (February 1952), 71 (Anon.)

1947

THREE CONCERT PIECES (Opus 31)
For piano, violin and cello

Moto Perpetuo (Allegro) [2'49"]
Nocturne (Adagio, ma appassionato) [7'22"]
Alla Bulgharese (Allegro) [5'24"]

Commissioned by: The London International Trio
Dedication: "To the London International Trio"
First performance: London, Wigmore Hall, 13 February 1948
  The London International Trio: Tom Bromley (piano),
  Jan Sedivka (violin) and Sela Trau (cello)
First broadcast performance: BBC Third Programme, 14 June 1960.
  The Reizenstein Trio
Publication: Novello & Co. Ltd. Score and parts © 1965
Manuscript: Whereabouts unknown
Recordings: Meridian Records CDE 84458 (2002). Adam

Summerhayes (violin), Catherine Summerhayes (piano) and
Joseph Spooner (cello)
Bibliography: *Musical Times*, 89 (March 1948), 91 (Anon.); *Musical
Times*, 92 (September 1951), 415-16 (C. Mason)

MACBETH
Incidental music (for chamber orchestra, with settings of the song-texts) to
the play by William Shakespeare
Directed by Norris Houghton
Commissioned by: Michael Redgrave

picc.0.3.1/2.3.3.0/timpani/percussion/harp/strings (2.0.3.1)

First performance: London, Aldwych Theatre, 18 December 1947
  Music played by 23 session musicians, conducted by Lehman
  Engel. The music was pre-recorded by the Special Recording
  Department of the EMI Studios Ltd. A schedule of records
  reveals that the music was recorded on 21 October 1947, in
  two sessions. Twenty-one numbers were recorded, a total of 14'05"
Cast included Michael Redgrave, Douglas Wilmer, Leslie Sands and
  Rupert Davies
Unpublished
Manuscript: British Library, London. MS Mus. 410: sSort score in ink.
  Two schedules of the music exist, one act by act, scene by
  scene, the other a schedule of "re-orchestrated" music, divided into
  two parts: Act 1-Act 3, scene 4, and Act 4, scene 1-Act 5, scene 6
  (BL Deposit 2005/32)
Bibliography: Strachen, A. *Secret Dreams: The Biography of Michael
  Redgrave*. London, Weidenfeld & Nicolson, 2004, 247-251.
  The *London Evening Standard*, 20 February 1948, 6 (M. Shulman);
  The Tatler and Bystander, 7 January 1948, 7 (A. Cookman); *The
  Times*, 19 December 1947, 6 (Anon.)

LIDICE
Song for unaccompanied mixed chorus (SATB)
Text: Nancy Bush

Duration: 4'
First performance: Lidice, Prague Radio, ? August 1947
  WMA Singers, conducted by Alan Bush
First British performance: London, King George's Hall, 16 June 1949
  WMA Singers, conducted by Aubrey Bowman

Publication: Workers' Music Association. Vocal score © 1947
Manuscript: Whereabouts unknown
Note: This song recalls the crime committed by German occupying forces
  on 10 June 1942 when Lidice (Czechoslovakia) was destroyed
  and its inhabitants murdered or sent to concentration camps in
  revenge for the killing of Reinhard Heydrich

1948

COMMUNIST MANIFESTO CENTENARY MEETING AND PAGEANT
Script by Montagu Slater with music for military band and
mixed chorus (SATB)

Music and arrangements by various composers including Rutland
Boughton, Christian Darnton, Inglis Gundry, Phillip Cardew, Malcolm
Arnold, Aubrey Bowman, Bernard Stevens and Alan Bush who arranged
music for the Finale (No. 15) comprising:

A. The People's Flag (words: Jim Connell – Tune: Maryland)
  Arranged for mixed chorus (SATB)
B. The Internationale (words from the French: Eugene Pottier-Tune by
  Pierre Degeyter)
  Arranged for mixed chorus (SATB) and military band

First performance: London, Royal Albert Hall, 30 March 1948
  Birmingham Clarion Singers and The London Communist
  Choir with military band, conducted by Alan Bush
Publication of *The International* only: Workers' Music Association
  Vocal score © 1948
Manuscript: British Library, London. MS Mus. 411, ff. 74-91 and 413:
  Score in ink. Add. MS 69024, ff. 38-42 is an autograph piano
  score of the same music
Bibliography: The Programme Book for the Pageant

OUR SONG
For mezzo-soprano or baritone solo, mixed chorus (SATB) and piano
Text: Nancy Bush

Commissioned for the opening of the Nottingham Co-operative Arts Centre
Duration: 3′
First performance: Nottingham, Arts Centre Theatre, 7 November 1948

Nottingham Co-operative Arts Centre Choir and Alan Bush
(piano), conducted by David Ellenberg
First London performance: King George's Hall, 16 June 1949
Esther Salaman (mezzo-soprano) and the WMA Singers with
Alan Bush (piano), conducted by David Ellenberg
Publication: WMA Vocal score © 1948. Reprinted 1970 in *Songs of
Struggle*
Manuscript: British Library, London. MS. Mus 416, ff. 77-86: Full score
in ink; sketches in Deposit 2005/32

1948-1950

WAT TYLER
Opera in two acts with prologue
Libretto by Nancy Bush
Commissioned by: The Arts Council of Great Britain in the 1951 Festival
of Britain Opera Competition

Principals: Herdsman *bass*, Escaped Serf *tenor*, Fishwife *mezzo-soprano*,
Elderly Peasant *tenor*, Wat Tyler *baritone*, Herald *tenor*, Sir
Thomas Hampton *bass-baritone*, Clerk *tenor*, Retainer *tenor*,
Jennet, daughter of Wat Tyler *soprano*, Margaret, wife of Wat
Tyler *lyric soprano*, John Ball, a Priest *bass*, Minstrel *tenor*,
King Richard II *tenor*, Eleanor, the Queen Mother *mezzo-
soprano*, Earl of Salisbury *baritone*, Walworth, Lord Mayor of
London *bass-baritone*, Archbishop Sudbury *bass*
Chorus of Peasants, Townsfolk, Nobles

3.2.2.3/4.3.3.1/timpani/percussion(2)/harp/strings (+ 2 stage trumpets)

Dedication (added to the printed copy in 1974): "To Hyman Fagan, author
of the historical study *Nine Days that Shook England*, whose
instigation and encouragement led me to write the work"
Duration: 135'15"
Performance history:

First (concert) performance: London, Salle Erard, 26 November 1950
Soloists with the WMA Singers, the Radlett Singers and the
WMA Opera Group with Alan Bush (piano), conducted by
Bernard Stevens and John Myers
A further performance of excerpts was performed in honour of Alan

Bush's 50th birthday: London, Conway Hall, 15 December 1950
(Presented by the Workers' Musical Association)
First broadcast performance: Berlin, Berliner Rundfunk, 3 April 1952
Symphony Orchestra and Chorus of the Berliner Rundfunk,
conducted by Alan Bush (sung in German). Repeated on 11
April 1952
First staged performance: Leipzig, Opera House, 6 September 1953
Soloists with the Leipzig Opera Chorus and Gewandhaus
Orchestra, conducted by Helmut Seidelmann
Produced by Heinrich Voigt
Further performance: Rostock, Opera House, 1955. Conducted by
Hans Gahlenbeck
First broadcast performance in the UK: BBC, Third Programme, 9
December 1956 (and repeated 10 December 1956)
Soloists with the BBC Chorus and Royal Philharmonic Orchestra,
conducted by Stanford Robinson
Further performance in Germany: Magdeburg, Opera House, 1959
Conducted by Gottfried Schwiers
First staged performance in the UK: London, Sadler's Wells Theatre,
19 June 1974
Soloists with the Keynote Opera Chorus and Royal Philharmonic
Orchestra, conducted by Stanford Robinson
Produced by Tom Hawkes

Publication: Henschelverlag, Berlin. Vocal score © 1954 (German);
Novello, London. Vocal score © 1959 (German/English)
1959 (German and English)
Libretto: J. Williams Ltd. © 1956
Manuscript: British Library, London. MS. Mus. 367-370: Draft short score,
in pencil, with occasional annotations in ink; 371, 372: Vocal
score- *copies* of the ink score of the piano reduction, with
autograph title pages; 373-376: Full score in ink
Bibliography: Dent, E.J. 'Wat Tyler' *in* WMA. Tribute to Alan
Bush on his 50th birthday: A symposium. London, WMA, 1950, 49-52;
R. O'Higgins: 'The English Production of Wat Tyler, June
1974' Alan Bush Music Trust website;
H. Pischner: 'Working on Opera with Bush in Germany' *in*
Stevenson, R.(ed.) Time Remembered Alan Bush: a symposium.
Kidderminster, Bravura Publications, 1981, 89
British Music Society Newsletter, No. 84 (December 1999),
369 (R. O'Higgins); *Composer*, No. 51 (Spring 1974), 5

(B. Stevens); *The Listener*, 56 (6 December 1956), 965
(E. Chapman); *The Manchester Guardian*, 11 December 1956, 5
(W.L.Waterhouse); *Music and Musicians*, 22 (June 1974),
 7-8 (Anon.); *Music and Musicians*, 22 (August 1974), 34-35
(F.G. Barker); *Musical Opinion*, 75 (January 1952), 231
(E.J. Dent); *Musical Times*, 92 (January 1951), 36 (A. Jacobs);
Musical Times, 92 (February 1951), 84 (A. Jacobs); *Musical
Times*, 93 (May 1952), 215-216 (W.R.Anderson); *Musical
Times*, 94 (June 1953), 263-264 (W.R Anderson); *Musical
Times*, 95 (February 1954), 67 (Anon.); *Musical Times*, 97
(December 1956), 633-636 (H. Ottaway); *Musical Times*, 115
(August 1974), 677 (W. Dean); *Opera* 4 (December 1953), 743
(Anon.); *Opera* 8 (February 1957), 1-2 (J. Amis); *Opera* 25
(August 1974), 739-740 (A. Blyth); *Tempo*, No. 110 (September
1974), 44-45 (C. McDonald); *The Times*, 1 July 1950, 6 (Anon.);
The Times, 27 September 1952, 8 (Anon.)

OTHER VERSIONS

(1) **Wat Tyler's Meditation** (Act 1, Scene 2)
Arranged for voice with piano duet by the composer
Unpublished
Manuscript: British Library, London. MS. Mus.372, ff. 99-102: Score in
ink

(2) **John Ball's Scene** (Act 1, Scene 3)
Arranged for bass, mixed chorus (SATB), piano and organ by the composer
Unpublished
Manuscript: British Library, London.MS.Mus.372, ff. 103-113: Score in
ink

1949

SYMPHONY No. 2 'THE NOTTINGHAM' (Opus 33)
For orchestra
In four movements

(1) Sherwood Forest (Moderato-Allegro vivace) [9'19"]
(2) Clifton Grove (Largo) [11'13"]
(3) Castle Rock (Allegro molto) [5'30"]
(4) Goose Fair (Allegro moderato) [12'18"]

Commissioned by: The Nottingham Co-operative Society in celebration of the 500th anniversary of the founding of the city

2.2.2.2/4.3.3.1/timpani/percussion/strings

First performance: Nottingham, Albert Hall, 27 June 1949
  The London Philharmonic Orchestra, conducted by David
  Ellenberg
First broadcast performance: BBC Third Programme, 19 June 1951
  The London Philharmonic Orchestra, conducted by Clarence
  Raybould
First London performance: London Contemporary Music Centre,
  20 June 1951
  The London Philharmonic Orchestra, conducted by Clarence
  Raybould
First (concert) London performance: Royal Festival Hall, 11 December
  1952
  The London Philharmonic Orchestra, conducted by Adrian Boult
Publication: Joseph Williams Ltd. Full score © 1949
Manuscript (full score): Whereabouts unknown
  Working sketches of the Symphony (M7677) and a written
  introduction to the Symphony by the composer (M24,231) were
  presented to the Nottinghamshire Archives by Alan Bush
Recordings: Olufsen Records CLASSCD 484 (recorded February 2004)
  Royal Northern College of Music [Manchester] Symphony
  Orchestra, conducted by Douglas Bostock
Bibliography: Ellenberg, D. 'The Form of the Nottingham Symphony' in
  WMA, Tribute to Alan Bush on his 50th birthday: A symposium.
  London, WMA, 1950, 45-48;
  Russell, T. 'The Nottingham Symphony' in
  WMA. Tribute to Alan Bush on his 50 birthday: A symposium.
  London, WMA, 1950, 40-44;
  BMS Newsletter, No. 81 (March 1999), 276-7 (M. Hinson);
  London Philharmonic Post, 6 No. 7 (November-December
  1952), 81-82 (Anon.); *Musical Opinion*, 76 (January 1953), 201
  (Anon.); *Musical Times*, 90 (August 1949), 283-5 (W.R.
  Anderson); *Musical Times*, 90 (August 1949), 290 (A. Jacobs);
  Musical Times, 92 (August 1951), 370 (C. Mason); *Musical
  Times*, 93 (December 1952), 552-553 (W.R. Anderson); *Musical
  Times*, 94 (February 1953), 82 (Anon.); *Musical Times*, 131
  (October 1990), 560 (A. Cross); *Strad*, 63 (January 1953), 267

(Anon.); *The Times*, 12 December 1952, 12 (Anon.)
Note: A set of *Nottingham Fanfares* for brass also exists
  (copies of the parts in the Histon archive). They may have
  been used after the performance when the manuscript was
  formerly presented to the Lord Mayor

SONG OF FRIENDSHIP (Opus 34)
Cantata for bass solo, mixed chorus (SATB) and piano or orchestra
Text: Nancy Bush

Written for the British Soviet Friendship Society
2.0.3 + 2 sax.1/0.3.4.1/timpani/percussion
Duration: 11'
First performance: London, Empress Hall, 6 November 1949
  Soloist, WMA choir and orchestra, conducted by Alan Bush
Publication: Workers' Music Association Vocal score © 1949
Manuscript: British Library, London. MS. Mus.416, ff. 87-106: Full score
  in ink with corrections in red crayon. Sketches in Deposit 2005/32
  Text in German, with Czech and Dutch translations

1950

THE DREAM OF LLEWELYN AP GRUFFYDD (Opus 35)
For male voice chorus (TTBB) and piano
Text: Randall Swingler
Welsh text by Wil Ifan

Dedication: "To the Treorchy and District Male Voice Choir"
Duration: 8'
First performance: Treorchy (South Wales), Park & Dare Workman's Hall,
  11 April 1952
  Treorchy and District Male Voice Choir and Tom Jones (piano),
  conducted by John H. Davies
Publication: Joseph Williams Ltd. Vocal score (English and Welsh) © 1951
  Tonic sol fa edition: J.Williams Ltd. © 1952
Manuscript: Whereabouts unknown
Bibliography: *Music and Letters*, 32 (October 1951), 386-7 (Anon.)

THE PEOPLE'S PAPER
Song for soloist, mixed chorus and orchestra
Written to celebrate the 21st anniversary of *The Daily Worker*
  (The Peoples' Paper)

Text: Randall Swingler

First performance: London, Harringay Arena, 12 February 1950
  Choir and Orchestra, conducted by Alan Bush
Unpublished
Manuscript: British Library, London. MS. Mus. 424, ff. 51-52
Bibliography: *The Times*, 13 December 1950, 4 (Anon.)

TIMES OF DAY: A Little Suite for Piano
Four piano pieces for children

1.   Wake Up! (Allegro)
2.   Noon Ramble (Moderato)
3.   After School (Allegro moderato ma energico)
4.   Bedtime (Andante con moto)

Duration: 8′
First performance: Unable to trace
Publication: Joseph Williams Ltd. Score © 1950
Manuscript: Whereabouts unknown

SHINING VISION: SONG FOR PEACE
For mixed chorus (SATB) and piano
Text: Montagu Slater

First performance: London, Conway Hall, 15 December 1956
  The WMA Singers with Alan Bush (piano)
Publication: Workers' Music Association. Vocal score © 1950
  Kahn & Averill for the WMA 1989 (in a collection of
  Peace Songs ed. John Jordan)
  Also published in Moscow 1963 (for baritone solo only)
Manuscript: British Library, London. MS. Mus. 422, ff. 59-60

1951

TRENT'S BROAD REACHES (Opus 36)
For horn (in F) and piano
Written as a tribute to Noel Mewton-Wood

Duration: 4′
First performance: London, Wigmore Hall, 28 January 1955
  Dennis Brain (horn) and Alan Bush (piano)

(A concert in memory of Noel Mewton-Wood)
Publication: Schott & Co. Score and part © 1952
Manuscript: Whereabouts unknown. Working sketch (M7678) presented to
  Nottinghamshire Archive by the composer
Bibliography: *Musical Times*, 96 (March 1955), 151 (D. Mitchell);
  The Times, 29 January 1955, 8 (Anon.)

HIROSHIMA – SIX YEARS AFTER
Music for a news feature

Commissioned by the BBC
Instrumentation: Flute and harp
Feature first shown: London, BBC Television, 15 August 1951
  Shown as part of an extended news bulletin on BBC Television
  Unable to trace the performers
Unpublished
Manuscript: Whereabouts unknown

TWO EASY PIECES
For cello and piano

(1) Song across the Water (Moderato) [2'01"]
(2) Fireside Story (Allegretto) [1'35"]

First performance: Unable to trace
Publication: Joseph Williams Ltd. Score and parts © 1952 (cello part edited
  by Herbert Withers)
Manuscript: British Library, London. MS. Mus. 353, ff. 23-27: Score and
  cello parts for the two pieces in ink
Recordings: Meridian Records CDE 84458 (2002). Joseph Spooner (cello)
  and Catherine Summerhayes (piano)

1952

CONCERT SUITE (Opus 37)
For cello and orchestra

(1) Introduction (Molto lento)
(2) Divisions on a Ground (Moderato)
(3) Ballett (Allegro vivace)
(4) Poem (Molto lento)
(5) Dance (Allegro energico ma non troppo)

2.2.2.2/4.2.3.0/timpani/percussion/harp/strings

Duration: 28'
First performance: Budapest, 1952
  Vera Denes (cello) and the Budapest Philharmonic Orchestra,
  conducted by Alan Bush
First broadcast performance: BBC Third Programme, 14 October 1953
  Zara Nelsova (cello) /BBC Symphony Orchestra, conducted by
  Alan Bush
First public performance: Royal Albert Hall, 7 September 1956
  Florence Hooton (cello) with the BBC Symphony Orchestra,
  conducted by Alan Bush
Publication: Joseph Williams Ltd. Score © 1957
Manuscript: British Library, London. MS. Mus. 340, ff. 1-82: Full score in
  ink with conductor's markings in red crayon; sketches in Deposit
  2005/32
Bibliography: *Musical Opinion*, 80 (June 1957), 537 (Anon.); *Musical
  Times*, 94 (December 1953), 570 (A. Frank); *Musical Times*, 97
  (November 1956), 596 (D. Mitchell)

OTHER VERSIONS

Arrangement for cello and piano
by the composer

Publication: J. Williams Ltd. Score and part © 1957

DEFENDER OF PEACE (Opus 39)
Character Study for Orchestra (a re-composition of the last movement of
Symphony No. 1 (Opus 21))

2.2.2.2/4.3.3.1/timpani/percussion (1)/piano/strings

Duration: 5'45"
First performance: Vienna Radio broadcast, 24 May 1952
  Orchestra, conducted by Alan Bush
First public performance: Moscow Youth Festival, 1957
  Orchestra, conducted by Alan Bush
Publication: Soviet Music Publishers, Moscow. Full score © 1966
Manuscript: British Library, London. MS. Mus. 340, ff. 83-106:
  Full score in ink, with conductor's markings in red and blue crayon
  and pencil

THREE ENGLISH SONG-PRELUDES (Opus 40)
Arranged for organ

(1) Worldes blis ne last no throwe: 13th Century Song (Andante con moto)
(2) Be Merry: 15th Century Carol (Allegretto)
(3) Lowlands, my Lowlands: 17th Century Shanty (Tranquillo)

Duration: 8′
First performance: London, St. Mark's Church (North Audley Street),
  21 April 1954
  Caleb H. Trevor (organ)
First broadcast performance: BBC Third Programme, 21 April 1954
  Caleb H. Trevor (organ)
Publication: J. Williams Ltd. Score © 1954. Re-issued by Oxford
  University Press. Score © 1976
Manuscript: Whereabouts unknown. Sketches in BL Deposit 2005/32
Recordings: Pipework Records SCS 655 (© 2000)
  Robert Crowley (organ)
  (Recorded in St. Mary's Parish Church, Hitchin)
Bibliography: *Music and Letters*, 35 (July 1954), 263 (Anon.)

1953

VOICES OF THE PROPHETS (Opus 42)
Cantata for tenor voice and piano

(1) 'For behold, I create new heavens' (Isaiah, from ch. 65) (Con moto
    moderato, un poco largamente)
(2) 'So at length the spirit of man' (*Against the Scholastic Philosophy*,
    John Milton) (Allegro)
(3) 'Rouse up, O Young Man' (*Selections from Milton*, William Blake)
    (Allegro)
(4) 'My Song is for all Men' (Peter Blackman, 1952) (Allegro moderato,
    un poco largamente)

Dedication: "To Peter Pears and Noel Mewton-Wood"
Duration: 18′30″
First performance: London, Recital Room (Royal Festival Hall), 22 May
  1953
  Peter Pears (tenor) and Noel Mewton-Wood (piano)

First performance: BBC Third Programme, 9 January 1954
  Peter Pears (tenor) and Noel Mewton-Wood (piano)
Publication: Joseph Williams Ltd. Vocal score © 1953
Manuscript: Whereabouts unknown. Sketches in BL Deposit 2005/32
Recordings: Redcliffe Recordings RR 008 (1994). Philip Langridge
  (tenor) and Piers Lane (piano)
Bibliography: *Music and Letters*, 34 (October 1953), 349 (Anon.);
  Music and Letters, 35 (July 1954), 268-69 (Anon.); *Music Review*, 14
  (August 1953), 232 (Anon.); *Musical Opinion*, 76 (July 1953), 613
  (Anon.); *Musical Times*, 94 (November 1953), 514-16 (C. Mason);
  Musical Times, 136 (February 1995), 108 (W. Mellers); *Strad*, 67
  (May 1956), 3

THE SPELL UNBOUND
Operetta for girls' voices in an Elizabethan setting
Libretto by Nancy Bush

Of the 14 numbers in the score, the sources of the following are
indicated in the score: 1. [Overture] Sellenger's Round; 2. After
a galliard by John Bull; 3. Hunsdon House, a folk-dance; 4. After
an Elizabethan song by D. Shaw [?]; 5. Gay Gordon, a Scottish
Ballad; 6. Daphne, a country dance tune; 7. After an Elizabethan
song by John Dowland.
Scene 2-8. Adapted from a Sussex folk-song; 9. After the folk-
song 'The Beggar Boy'; 10. [nothing stated] 11. After an
Elizabethan pavane; 12. After an Elizabethan song by Thomas
Campion; 13. After an Elizabethan song by John Dowland; 14.
Finale: Sellenger's Round

Principals: Juliet, an Elizabethan girl; Mistress Trounce, her governess;
  Old Nurse; Audrey, a waiting maid; Moll Pavey, a village child;
  Girls of the household
  Chorus of Village Children

Time: The late sixteenth century

Scene 1. The garden of an English manor house, one June afternoon
Scene 2. A shuttered room in the house, the same night

Duration: 70'
First performance: Bournemouth School for Girls, 6 March 1955

The Ascham Choir, conducted by H.M. Hounsell with Marjorie
Martin (piano)
Publication: Novello & Co. Vocal score © 1954
Manuscript: Whereabouts unknown. Synopsis in BL Deposit 2005/32
Bibliography: *Music Clubs Magazine*, 34 (June 1955), 40 (Anon.);
  Notes, 12 (December 1954), 152 (Anon.)

THREE NORTHUMBRIAN IMPRESSIONS (Opus 42) [2nd use]
For Northumbrian small pipes

(1) Prelude (Moderato)
(2) Lament (Lento)
(3) Dance (Vivo): Based in the "Mitford Galloway"

Duration: 10'
First performance: London, Wigmore Hall, 28 October 1979
  Richard Butler (pipes)
First broadcast performance: BBC Radio 3, 13 July 1981
  Richard Butler (pipes)
Unpublished
Manuscript: British Library, London. MS. Mus. 353, ff. 28-31; sketches
  in Deposit 2005/32
Bibliography: C. Carver: 'Northumbrian Impressions". Alan Bush
  Music Trust website
Note: These pieces were written for Jack Armstrong, a Northumbrian
  pipes virtuoso, who met Alan Bush during the composition of
  Men of Blackmoor. Richard Butler was a pupil of Jack Armstrong

OTHER VERSIONS

Arrangement for oboe with piano accompaniment (Opus 42a)
by the composer

First performance: London, Arts Council Drawing Room, 14
  December 1953
  Joy Boughton (oboe) and Kenneth Baker (piano)
First broadcast performance: BBC Home Service, 13 February 1958
  Roger Lord (oboe) and Josephine Lee (piano)
Publication: Novello & Co. Ltd. Score and part © 1956
Bibliography: *Musical America*, 77 (June 1957), 28 (Anon.);
  Musical Opinion, 80 (March 1957), 347 (Anon); *Musical*

Times, 95 (February 1954), 92 (D. Mitchell); *The Times*, 15 December 1953, 10 (Anon.)

PAVANE FOR THE CASTLETON QUEEN (Opus 43)
For brass band

Written for the Castleton Wakes Committee and based on the Castleton Garland Dance and an Elizabethan Quodra Pavane

Solo cornet (Bb); soprano cornet (Eb); ripieno cornet (Bb) and flute; 2nd cornet (Bb); 3rd cornet (B flat); solo, 1st & 2nd horn in Eb; 1st baritone in Bb; 2nd baritone in Bb; 1st and 2nd trombone in Bb; bass trombone; euphonium in Bb; Eb bass; drums

Duration: 3'30"
First performance: Castleton (Derbyshire), sometime in 1953
  Castleton Brass Band, conducted by Alan Bush
Unpublished
Manuscript: Whereabouts unknown. Copy in the Histon Archive
  Sketches in BL Deposit 2005/32

THE BALLAD OF FREEDOM'S SOLDIER (Opus 44)
Cantata for tenor and bass-baritone soli, mixed chorus (SATB) and orchestra
Text: John Manifold, incorporating a poem by Khristo Botev

2.1+1.2.2/4.3.2+1.0/timpani/percussion/harp/strings

Dedication: "To the memory of Major Frank Thompson, British Military
  Mission, national hero of the People's Republic of Bulgaria"
Duration: 20'15"
First performance: Russe (Bulgaria), 5 April 1963
  Soloists and the Philharmonic de l'État, conducted by Ilya Temkov
First British performance: Battersea, Town Hall, 6 November 1975
  Robin Legate (tenor) and Andrew Golder (bass-baritone) with the
  Putney Choral Society and Orchestra, conducted by Stephen Rhys
Unpublished
Manuscript: British Library, London. MS. Mus. 417, ff. 1-25: Vocal score
  in ink with performance annotations in pencil; sketch in Deposit
  2005/32
Bibliography: *Musical Events*, 18 No. 5 (Mat 1963), 16 (Anon.)

1954

AUTUMN POEM (Opus 45)
For horn and piano
Written as a tribute to Noel Mewton-Wood
Duration: 3'50"
First performance: London, Wigmore Hall, 28 January 1955
  Dennis Brain (horn) and Alan Bush (piano)
Publication: Schott & Co. Ltd. Score and part © 1955
Manuscript: Whereabouts unknown
Bibliography: *Music Review*, 17 (August 1956), 259+262 (Anon.);
  Musical Opinion, 79 (December 1955), 155 (Anon.); *Musical
  Times*, 96 (March 1955), 151 (D. Mitchell); *The Times*, 29
  January 1955, 8 (Anon.)

1954-1955

MEN OF BLACKMOOR (Die Männer von Blackmoor)
Opera in three acts
Libretto by Nancy Bush with German translation by Marianne Graefe
Commissioned by: Leipzig Municipal Opera

Principals: Soldier *bass*, Sarah, Thomas's daughter *soprano*, Thomas, an
  older miner *bass*, Geordie, his friend *tenor*, Daniel, a young miner
  baritone, Jenny, Fletcher's daughter *mezzo-soprano*, Fletcher,
  Viewer of Blackmoor Pit *bass baritone*, Four soldiers *tenor*,
  tenor, baritone, bass, Leadminer *tenor*, Young leadminer, *bass*
  Chorus of miners and their wives, leadminers and soldiers
  3.3.3.3/4.3.3.1/timpani/percussion(2)/strings
Duration: 130'

Performance history:

First performance: Weimar, German National Theatre, 18 November 1956
  Soloists with the German National Opera Chorus and Gwandhaus
  Orchestra, conducted by Helmut Seyelmann.
  Produced by Alan Bush
A further new production: Jena, Opera House, 12 November 1957
  Same soloists and orchestra as in the Weimar production conducted
  by Alan Bush
First broadcast performance: Berlin, Berliner Rundfunk, 22 and 23 April
  1958

Further productions at the Leipzig Opera House on 5 October 1959 and the
Zwickau Opera House on 10 May 1960
First British stage performance: Amateur production at the Oxford
University Opera Club, 30 November–3 December 1960
Soloists and Oxford University Opera Orchestra, conducted by
Jack Westrup. Produced by Eddie Gilbert
First broadcast performance in the UK: BBC, Radio 3, 2 October 1969.
Soloists with the BBC Northern Singers and the BBC Northern
Symphony Orchestra, conducted by Stanford Robinson.
Produced by Ernest Warburton
(This was re-broadcast in December 1995 as a memorial tribute to
Alan Bush)

Publication: Henschelverlag, Berlin and Joseph Williams Ltd. Vocal score
© 1959 (English and German); Libretto: J. Williams Ltd. © 1959
Manuscript: British Library, London. MS. Mus. 377-379: Full score in ink;
sketch of Act III in Deposit 2005/32
Bibliography: *Music and Musicians*, 8 (July 1960), 19 (Anon.); *Music and
Musicians*, 9 (January 1961), 29+ (F. Dibb); *Musica*, 11 (January
1957), 29-30 (H.R. Jung); *Musical Opinion*, 83 (March 1960),
401 (Anon.); *Musical Opinion*, 84 (February 1961), 281-282
(R. Stuart); *Musical Times*, 98 (January 1957), 38 (E. Chapman);
Musical Times, 102 (January 1961), 25 (Anon.); *Opera* 8
(January 1957), 14+ (J. Amis); *Opera* 12 (February 1961), 137-139
Anon.); *Opera* 20 (December 1969), 110 (M. Rudland); *Score*
No. 13 (September 1955), 78 (Anon.); *The Times*, 1 December
1960, 7 (Anon.)

1955

VARIATION (2nd: Allegro Molto) as part of 'Diabelleries': variations for
instruments

At the suggestion of Ralph Vaughan Williams, eight British composers
contributed a set of variations on a theme attributed to Alfred Scott-Gatty
(1847-1918) entitled 'Where's My Little Basket Gone?' and orchestrated
by Vaughan Williams
Besides Bush, the other composers were Howard Ferguson (variation I),
Alan Rawsthorne (III), Elisabeth Lutyens (IV), Elizabeth
Maconchy (V), Gerald Finzi (VI), Grace Williams (VII) and Gordon
Jacob (Finale)

1.1.1.1/1.1.0.0/strings

Duration: 0'45"
First performance: London, Arts Council Drawing Room, 16 May 1955
  Macnaghten New Music Group Ensemble conducted by Iris Lemare
Unpublished
Manuscript: British Library, London. Add. MS 59809 which includes all
  the full scores and parts (some autograph, others in the hands of
  Anne Macnaghten and Richard Rodney Bennett). Bush's
  contribution can be found as ff. 9-12; sketches in Deposit 2005/32

1957

NOCTURNE (Opus 46)
For piano
Originally written as 'Variations, Nocturne and Finale'. Two movements
were withdrawn after the first performance (see below) and later revised as
*Variations, Nocturne and Finale on an English Sea-Song for Piano and
Orchestra* Opus 60 (1962) (see below)

Dedication: "Dedicated in friendship and admiration to Dr Thomas
  Armstrong"
Duration: 6'
First performance: London, Arts Council Drawing Room, 21 March 1958
  Edna Iles (piano)
First broadcast performance: BBC Home Service, 22 August 1959
  Edna Iles (piano)
Publication: Novello & Co. Ltd. Score © 1970
Manuscript: British Library, London. MS Mus. 353,ff. 32-73: Full score in
  ink (The *Nocturne* is missing from this manuscript)
Recordings: Altarus Records AIR-CD-9004 (1984-1993)
  Peter Jacobs (piano)
Bibliography: *Musical Times*, 99 (May 1958), 270 (Anon.); *Musical
  Times*, 136 (February 1995), 108 (W. Mellers)

REVISED VERSION (1962)

VARIATIONS, NOCTURNE AND FINALE ON AN ENGLISH SEA-SONG
['Blow ye winds'] (Opus 60)
Version for piano and orchestra

BALLADE VOM MARSCH AUF ALDERMASTON
For speaker, mixed chorus (SATB) and instrumental ensemble
Text: Armin Müller

Instrumentation: 2 horns, 2 trumpets, 2 guitars, percussion and
  double bass
Duration: 4'
First performance: Weimar, 1958
Manuscript: British Library, London. MS. Mus. 417, ff. 29-37:
  Full score in blue ink

OTHER VERSIONS

(1) Ballad of the March to Aldermaston

Version for speaker, mixed chorus (SATB) and instrumental ensemble
Text: Armin Müller. English version text: Nancy Bush

Instrumentation: 2 clarinets, 3 trumpets, tenor trombone, 3 guitars, piano,
  percussion and strings
First British performance: London, St. Pancras Town Hall, 1 April 1961
  Glyn Davies (speaker) with the combined Glasgow YCL and
  London choirs, instrumental ensemble, conducted by Alan Bush
Unpublished
Manuscript: British Library, London. MS. Mus.417, ff. 38-48: Score in ink

(2) The Ballad of Aldermaston

Version with accompaniment for piano and percussion

Unpublished
Manuscript: British Library, London. MS. Mus. 417, ff. 49-63: Score in ink

(3) Ballad of the March to Aldermaston

Unpublished
Manuscript: British Library London. MS. Mus. 417, ff. 64-74: Chorus part
  in ink

MISTER PLAYFORD'S TUNES (Opus 49)
A Little Suite for Piano
The tunes are taken from John Playford's *English Dancing Master* of 1651

1. Argeers (Allegro energico)
2. The Whish and Petters Black (Allegretto)
3. Nonesuch (Allegro)
4. The Beggar Boy (Allegretto)
5. The Slip, a going-out (Allegro vivace)

Duration: 5'
First performance: Unable to trace
Publication: Joseph Williams Ltd. Score © 1959
Manuscript: Whereabouts unknown

THE WORLD IS HIS SONG (Opus 51)
For solo bass, mixed chorus (SATB) and instrumental ensemble
Text: Nancy Bush

Instrumentation: 2 horns, 2 trumpets, 3 trombones, tuba, guitar,
  percussion and piano

Dedication: "To Paul Robeson"
Duration: 6'
First performance: London, Royal Albert Hall, 15 February 1959
  Martin Lawrence (bass-baritone), WMA Massed Choirs and
  Ensemble, conducted by Alan Bush (*The Daily Worker* Birthday
  Rally)
Unpublished
Manuscript: British Library, London. MS. Mus. 418, ff. 1-54: Full and
  vocal scores in ink

1959

DORIAN PASSACAGLIA AND FUGUE (Opus 52)
For orchestra

Introduction (Allegro) with 16 variations
Fugue (con moto moderato)

2+1.1.2.2+1/4.3.2+1.1/timpani/percussion(2)/strings

Duration: 16'30"
First performance: London, BBC Studios, 10 June 1961
  BBC Symphony Orchestra, conducted by Rudolf Schwarz
First public performance: Cheltenham, Town Hall, 14 July 1961

BBC Symphony Orchestra conducted by Rudolf Schwartz
(Broadcast in the BBC Home Service, direct from Cheltenham)
Publication: Novello & Co. Ltd. Score © 1962 (a facsimile of the
composer's autograph)
Manuscript: Whereabouts unknown
Bibliography: *The Times*, 15 July 1961, 4 (Anon.)

1959-1960

SYMPHONY No. 3 (The Byron Symphony) (Opus 53)
For orchestra
In four movements
Text (for the 4th movement, in Greek): Dionysos Solomos (from his
Ode on the Death of Lord Byron)

1. Newstead Abbey (a tempo molto moderato ma non lento)
2. Westminster (Tempo di marcia ceremoniale)
3. Il Palazzo Savioli (-)
4. Missolonghi (Moderato serioso)

Commissioned by: East German Radio

3.3.3.3/4.3.3.1/timpani/percussion/harp/strings (+ baritone and mixed
chorus (SATB) in the last movement)
Duration: 50′
First performance: Leipzig, Kongresshalle, 20 March 1962
Rudolf Lauhofer (baritone), Radio Chorus and Symphony
Orchestra of the GDR, conducted by Herbert Kegel
First British performance: London, Friends House, 6 June 1962
Noel Hewlett (baritone), Kensington Symphony Orchestra and
Chorus, conducted by Leslie Head
First broadcast performance: BBC Radio 3, 11 March 1973
Peter Walker (baritone), BBC Northern Singers and the BBC
Northern Symphony Orchestra, conducted by Bernard Keefe
Unpublished
Manuscript: British Library, London. MS. Mus. 341 (ff. 148): Draft score
in pencil, with a vocal score of the 4th movement in ink
Bibliography: *Hudebni Rozhledy* 15 (1962), 593 (W. Wolf); *Music and
Musicians*, 10 (June 1962), 32 (Anon.); *Music and Musicians*, 10
(July 1962), 45 (R. Angles); *Musical Events*, 17 (June 1962), 28
(Anon.); *Musical Events*, 17 (August 1962), 14 (A. Boyars);

Musical Opinion, 85 (August 1962), 648 (Anon.); *The Times*,
7 June 1962, 15 (Anon.)
Note: This symphony received the Handel Prize, presented by the City
Council of Halle in 1962

1960

ON LAWN AND GREEN (Opus 54) [formerly Suite für Cembale oder Klavier]
Suite for harpsichord or piano
In four movements

(1) Pavan (Moderato maestoso)
(2) Galliard (Allegro)
(3) Air (Andante parlando)
(4) Longway Set (Allegro vivace ma non troppo)

Dedication: "A present to my friend and colleague Hans Pischner as a
small recompense for his invaluable support and help eight years
ago. Radlett 1960"
Duration: 9′
First performance: Berlin, 1960
Hans Pischner (harpsichord)
First broadcast performance: London, BBC Studios, 12 October 1961
Millicent Silver (harpsichord)
Publication: Edition Peters, Leipzig. Score © 1962
Manuscript: British Library, London. Add. MS.59810, ff. 53-67: Sketches

TWO OCCASIONAL PIECES (Opus 56)
For organ

(1) For a Solemn Occasion (Andante serioso)
(2) For a Festal Occasion (Allegro moderato)

Dedication: "To C.H. Trevor" [printed copy only]
Duration: 9′
First performance: Unable to trace
Publication: Novello & Co. Ltd. Score © 1962 (*Original Compositions for
the Organ, new series 322*)
Manuscript: British Library, London. MS. Mus. 354, ff. 34-53: Score in ink
Recordings: Pipework Records SCS 655 (2000)
Robert Crowley (organ)
(Recorded in St. Mary's Parish Church, Hitchin)

OTHER VERSIONS

FOR A FESTAL OCCASION (Opus 58) [No. 2 of the above]
For organ and orchestra

2.2.2.2/4.2.3.0/timpani/percussion/strings (optional)
Duration: 5'
First performance: Hereford, Cathedral Church of the Blessed Virgin
  Mary and St. Ethelbert, 3 September 1961
  Peter Hurford (organ) and the London Symphony Orchestra,
  conducted by Melville Cook
Unpublished
Manuscript: British Library, London. MS. Mus. 354, ff. 54-70: Full score
  in ink
Bibliography: *Musical Times*, 103 (October 1961), 626 (E. Bradbury):
  The Times, 5 September 1961, 15 (Anon.)

THREE AFRICAN SKETCHES (Opus 55)
For flute with piano accompaniment, based on African melodies
Written for John Leach

(1)   Southern Rhodesia [later amended to Zimbabwe] (Allegro moderato)
(2)   (Igekle) Zululand [A Zulu tune] (Andante lentamente)
(3)   Congo (Allegro vivace)

Duration: 8'
First performance: London, Leighton House, 16 December 1960
  John Leach (flute) and Alasdair Graham (piano)
First broadcast performance: BBC, Broadcasting House, 2 April 1964
  Colin Chambers (flute) and Daphne Ibbott (piano)
  (Broadcast in the Home Service of the BBC)
Publication: Edition Peters, Leipzig. Score and part © 1962
Manuscript: British Library, London. MS .Mus. 354, ff. 1-33: Scores and
  flute parts in ink

1961

FOUR SEAFARERS' SONGS (Opus 57)
For baritone and piano accompaniment
Texts from the *Penguin Book of English Folk-songs*

1. The Ship in Distress (Allegro determinato)
2. Rataliff Highway (Allegro commodo)
3. The Greenland Fishery (Con moto moderato)
4. Jack the Jolly Tar (Allegro vivace moderato)

Duration: 11′
First performance: London, Morley College, 19 November 1961
  Philip Lewtas (baritone) and Alan Bush (piano)
Publication: Galliard Ltd. Vocal score © 1964
Manuscript: British Library, London. MS. Mus. 425, ff. 10-25
Recordings: Musaeus Recordings MZ CD 102 (2000). Paul Wilson
  (baritone) and Richard Black (piano)

THE TIDE THAT WILL NEVER TURN
A declaration by Hugh McDiarmid for two speakers, bass (or baritone),
mixed chorus (SATB), strings, percussion and piano
Written for the 27th National Congress of the Communist Party of
  Great Britain

1. Allegro moto e appasionate
1a. -
2. a tempo primo
3. Moderato
3a. -
4. Allegro moderato
5. Moderato
6. Allegro come primo

Duration: 15′
First performance: London, St. Pancras Town Hall, 1 April 1961
  Marjorie Mason and Glyn Davys (speakers), Martin Lawrence
  (bass), the Glasgow YCL Choir and WMA Massed Choirs,
  orchestra with Glyn Davys (piano), conducted by Alan Bush
Unpublished
Manuscript: British Library, London. MS. Mus. 418, ff. 55-105: Full score
  and parts in ink

THE FERRYMAN'S DAUGHTER
An opera of the Thames waterside for schools
Libretto by Nancy Bush

Principals: Mr Wilkins, an old waterman; Jenny, his daughter; Nat, a

young waterman; Tom Starling, a young farmer; Mrs Patchett, a
fisherman's wife
Chorus of watermen, fishermen and girls

Time: The eighteenth century

Scene 1:   The Thames at Wapping Old Stairs
Scene 2:   The same, three weeks later

Duration: c. 60'
First performance: Letchworth (Herts), St. Christopher School,
  6 March 1964. Musical producer: Austin O'Neill. Produced by
  Reginald Snell
Publication: Novello & Co. Ltd. Vocal score © 1963
Manuscript: Whereabouts unknown

THREE RÂGA MELODIES (Opus 59)
For unaccompanied solo violin

(1)   Himavirdani Râga (Con moto quasi allegro, ma poco agitato) [4'01"]
(2)   Nadatha-Rangini Râga (Allegretto grazioso) [1'54"]
(3)   Garudavirdani Râga (Dramatico e libramente, non adagio) [3'38"]

First performance: Bracknell, South Hill Park Arts Centre, 25 April 1980
  Hazel Smith (violin)
Publication: Galliard Ltd./Galaxy Music (New York) Score © 1969
Manuscript: Whereabouts unknown
Recordings: Meridian Records CDE 84481 (2004)
  Adam Summerhayes (violin)
Bibliography: *Strad*, 92 (May 1981), 3 (Anon.)
Note: Alan Bush wrote these as part of his preparations for *The Sugar
  Reapers*

SONG OF THE COSMONAUT
For baritone solo, mixed chorus and piano
Text: Miles Tomalin

Dedicatee: "To Major Yuri Gagarin"
Duration: 3'
First performance: Unable to trace
Publication: WMA Vocal score © 1963
Manuscript: British Library, London. MS. Mus. 423, ff. 1-14. Score in ink,

signed by Yuri Gagarin and dated 13 July 1961
Note: Major Gagarin visited the UK on 11, 12 and 13 July 1961 when a
reception in his honour was held for him in London

OTHER VERSIONS

'Working orchestration by the composer'
Scoring of the chorus part only for flute, recorder, 2 oboes, 3 clarinets, 2
  trombones, percussion, accordion and piano
Unpublished
Manuscript: British Library, London. MS Mus. 423, ff. 12-14

1962-1965

THE SUGAR REAPERS [originally **Guyana Johnny**]
Opera in two acts
Libretto by Nancy Bush
Commissioned by: Karl Keyser

Principals: Johnny Lucas, African sugar worker *bass*, Joseph, his
  younger brother *tenor*, Panasar, Indian sugar worker *tenor*,
  Ganesh Maraj, Indian overseer on the plantation *bass-baritone*,
  Mr R. Souza, keeper of the local rum shop *tenor*, Aaron, Johnny's
  10-yearold brother *non-singing*, Sumintra, Panasar's daughter
  soprano, Mrs. Lucas, Johnny's mother *mezzo-soprano*, Ella, an
  African village girl *soprano*, Another African village girl *contralto*,
  An Indian girl, A young African, A young Indian sugar-worker,
  "Captain", Local police sergeant, African *bass*, Police officer
  from Georgetown *baritone*, An Indian Priest, Dealers, Radio
  Announcer
Chorus of sugar-workers, villagers, policemen, girls and young
  men
3.3.3.3. (+ alto/ten.sax.)/ 4.3.3.1/timpani/percussion(2)/guitar(2)/ piano/
  harp/strings

Duration: 145′
First performance: Leipzig Opera House, 11 December 1966
  Soloists with the Leipzig Gewandhaus Orchestra and Leipzig
  Opera Chorus, conducted by Rolf Reuter
First broadcast performance: Leipzig, GDR Radio Production. Recorded 29
  January 1968
Two further performances: Tartu, Opera House, 1 November 1969

and Odessa, Opera House, 10 August 1973
First British (broadcast) performance: BBC Radio 3, 24 September 1976
  (A recording of the Leipzig performance)

Publication: Henschelverlag, Berlin.Vocal score © 1965 as *Guyana Johnny*
Manuscript: British Library, London. MS. Mus. 380-387:
  380-82: Draft score in pencil; 383: Vocal score in ink; 384-87:Full score
  in ink
Bibliography: K. Ird "Producing a Bush Opera in Estonia" *in* Stevenson,
  R. (ed.), Time Remembered. Kidderminster, Bravura, 1981, 92-94;
  Musik und Gesellschaft, 17 (May 1967), 320-2 (H. Schaefer);
  Music and Life, No. 33 (January 1967), 7-8 (J. Miller); *Music and
  Life*, No. 33 (January 1967), 8-9; *Music and Life*, No. 33 (January
  1967), 10-11 (M. Talbot); *Opera*, 18 (February 1967), 113-115
  (T. Armstrong); *Opera*, 30 (September 1979), 912-913 (E. Forbes);
  Royal Academy of Music Magazine, No. 192 (Midsummer 1967),
  17 and 19 (A. Bush); *Sovetskaya Muzyka*, 34 (July 1970), 55-58;
  The Times, 28 September 1965, 13 (Anon.); *USSR Union of
  Composers Information Bulletin*, No. 10 (1973), 12-13 (Anon.)

1963

DURING MUSIC (Opus 62)
Part-song for unaccompanied mixed chorus (SATB)
Text: Dante Gabriel Rossetti
Specially written for the Wood Green Arts Festival

Duration: 2'30"
First performance: London, Wood Green, 4 April 1964
  Choir from Alexandra Choral Society with local choirs and
  Geoff Vince (piano), conducted by Alan Bush
Publication: Novello & Co. Ltd. Vocal score © 1964
  Printed as a supplement in *Musical Times* (MT 1454) in
  April 1964
Manuscript: British Library, London. MS.Mus. 423, ff. 15-22: Draft
  score in pencil

1963-1964

PRELUDE, AIR AND DANCE (Opus 61)
For solo violin with accompaniment for string quartet and percussion

Based in part on Northumbrian folk-songs

Prelude (Allegretto un poco agitato)
Air
Dance (Allegro vivace)

Commissioned by the BBC in 1963, for the Tuesday Invitation Concerts
Duration: 14'30"
First performance: BBC, Broadcasting House, 28 April 1964
  Ralph Holmes (violin), the Aeolian String Quartet and Eric Allen
  (percussion), conducted by Alan Bush (Broadcast in the BBC's
  Third Programme)
Publication: Novello & Co. Ltd. Score © 1965. Violin part edited by Ralph
  Holmes
Manuscript: British Library, London. MS. Mus. 355, ff. 1-87: Score in ink
  and draft short score in pencil with annotations in ink
Bibliography: *Musical Times*, 105 (June 1964), 447 (P.J. Pirie); *The Times*,
  29 April 1964, 8 (Anon.)

OTHER VERSIONS

Arrangement for solo violin with piano accompaniment
by the composer
Violin part edited by Ralph Holmes

Publication: Novello & Co. Score © 1965

1965

PARTITA CONCERTANTE (Opus 63)
For orchestra
In four movements

(1) Overture (Maestoso)
(2) Hornpipe (Allegro moderato)
(3) Air (Allegretto)
(4) Cheviot Reel (Allegro)

2.1.2.1/2.2.1.0/timpani/percussion(2)/piano/strings
Duration: 12'30"
First documented performance: Dartford, North West Kent College of
  of Technology, ? May 1975.

The Dartford Symphony Orchestra, conducted by Leonard Davis
Publication: Novello & Co. Ltd. Full score © 1966
Manuscript: Whereabouts unknown

TWO DANCES FOR CIMBALOM [Két Tànc Cimbalomra] (Opus 64)

Specially commissioned for a concert by the British Hungarian Friendship
Society to celebrate the twentieth anniversary of the liberation of Hungary

Dedication: "To John Leach"
Duration: 7′
First performance: London, Arts Council Drawing Room, 10 March 1965
  John Leach (cimbalom)
Publication: Zenemű kiadó Vállalat, Budapest. Score © 1966 (edited by
  John Leach)
Manuscript: British Library, London. MS. Mus. 356, ff. 1-8: Score in ink

1966-1968

JOE HILL: THE MAN WHO NEVER DIED
Opera in two acts
Libretto by Barrie Stavis after his play *The Man Who Never Died*
Commissioned by: The Berlin State Opera

Principals: Joe Hill *baritone*, Ed Rowan *baritone* and Ben Winton *tenor*,
  Joe's Union friends, Tom Sharpe, a false friend *tenor*, Policeman
  baritone, Isadore Rabinowitz *baritone*, Another speaker *baritone*,
  Harry Macrae, private detective *tenor*, Adam Steele, his assistant
  tenor, John Moody, copper-mine owner *bass*, Paul Blake, Police
  Chief *baritone*, Hilda Winton, Ben's wife *mezzo-soprano*, Italian
  worker *tenor*, Greek worker *baritone*, Martha Weber, Joe's girl
  soprano, Harry Weber, her husband *bass*, Policemen *tenor* and
  bass
Additional characters in Act 2:
  Mike Daly, a prison guard *bass*, Scott McBride, a crooked lawyer
  bass, District Attorney *bass*, Judge Mitchell *tenor*, Witness, *mezzo-
  soprano*, Alexander Marshall, Joe Hill's attorney *bass*, Members of
  the Board of Pardons *tenor*, *baritone*, *bass*, Cowboy *tenor*,
  Reverend White *tenor*, Engineer *baritone* and William Weed,
  Governor of Utah *baritone*
2.3.3+1.2/.4.3.3.1/timpani/percussion(2)/accordion/harp/piano/strings

Duration: 130'
First performance: East Berlin, German State Opera House, 29 September
1970. Soloists with the Berlin Opera Chorus and Berlin State Opera
Orchestra, conducted by Heinz Fricke (East Berlin Arts Festival)
First British (broadcast) performance: BBC Radio 3, 29 July 1976
Soloists with the BBC Singers and the BBC Concert Orchestra,
conducted by James Judd

Unpublished
Manuscript: British Library, London. MS. Mus. 388-393:
388, 389-draft score in pencil (388 contains three different versions
of the end of Act 1, the third a *photocopy* of a *copyist's* vocal score
in German); 390-391-vocal score in ink; 392-392-full score in ink
Bibliography: Stavis, B. 'A History-A Portrait-A Memory' *in* Stevenson,
R. (ed.), Time Remembered. Kidderminster, Bravura, 1981, 95-110
Christian Science Monitor, 63 (2 November 1970), 4
(J.H. Sutcliffe); *Composer*, No. 38 (Winter 1970-71), 36 (Anon.);
Hudebni Rozhledy 24, No. 4 (1971). 164-165 (V. Pospisil);
Musik und Gesellschaft, 20 (December 1970), 854-856
(L. Markowski); *Oper u Konzert*, 8 (December 1970), 4 (Anon.);
Opera, 30 (September 1979), 912-13 (E. Forbes); *Opera News*,
35 (5 December 1970), 30 (J.H. Sutcliffe); *Opern Welt* (Yearbook,
1971), 99 (Anon.); *Sovetskaya Muzyka*, 35 (May 1971), 115-
117 (V. Fere); *World Music*, 13, No. 1 (1971), 75 (Anon.)

1967

SUITE FOR TWO PIANOS (Opus 65)
In five movements

(1) Prologue (Moderato)
(2) Volga Harvest (Allegro vivace)
(3) Kinloch Iorram (Allegro tempestoso ma non presto)
(4) Samarkand Dugokh (Allegro grazioso)
(5) Pennine Round (Allegro vivace ma non troppo)

Duration: 19'30"
First performance: London, Queen Elizabeth Hall, 23 September 1967
John Ogdon and Brenda Lucas (pianos)
(A concert organised by the Society for Cultural Relations
with the USSR. The work was written for this concert)

First broadcast performance: BBC Radio 3, 4 April 1969
  John Ogdon and Brenda Lucas (pianos)
Unpublished
Manuscript: British Library, London. MS. Mus. 356, ff. 9-50: Score in
  ink with a list of the sources of the folk-melodies employed in the Suite
Bibliography: *Musical Times*, 108 (November 1967), 1020-21
  (R. Henderson); *The Times*, 25 September 1967, 6 (W. Mann)

1968

THE ALPS AND ANDES OF THE LIVING WORLD (Opus 66)
Cantata for speaker, tenor solo, mixed chorus (SATB) and orchestra
Texts: *Hamlet* (Shakespeare), *Man's Place in Nature* (T.H. Huxley) and
April the Twelfth, 1961 (Nancy Bush)

Commissioned by: The Dartington Summer School, 1968

0.0.0.0/4.3.3.1/percussion/piano/strings (2/1/2/0)

Duration: 11'
First performance: Dartington, Dartington Hall, 9 August 1968
  John Amis (speaker), Joseph Ward (tenor), Summer School Choir
  and Ensemble including the Devon Brass Consort, with
  Alan Bush (piano), conducted by Philip Simms
First public performance: Newcastle upon Tyne, King's Hall (Newcastle
  University), 3 March 1972
  Ken Christie (speaker), Kenneth Ormston (tenor), City of
  Newcastle College of Education Choir and the New Tyneside
  Orchestra, with Alan Bush (piano), conducted by Stephen Pettit
Unpublished
Manuscript: British Library, London. MS.Mus.419 (ff. 21): Full score
  in ink
Bibliography: *Newcastle Evening Chronicle*, 3 March 1972, 12 (Anon.)

TIME REMEMBERED (Opus 67)
A Piece for Chamber Orchestra

Commissioned by: The 1969 Cheltenham International Festival of Music

1.1.1.1/1.0.0.0/harp/strings (2.1.1.1)

Dedication: "To Nancy Bush"
Duration: 11'30"
First performance: Cheltenham, Town Hall, 8 July 1969
  Melos Ensemble, conducted by Alan Bush
Unpublished
Manuscript: British Library, London. MS. Mus.343, (ff. 56): Sketches,
  short score (in ink) and draft full score (in pencil)
Bibliography: *Music and Musicians*, 18 (September 1969), 30-31
  (K. Dommett); *Musical Opinion*, 92 (September 1969), 631 (E.M.
  Webster)

1969

SCHERZO (Opus 68)
For wind orchestra with percussion
Based on an African melody sung in Guyana

Commissioned by: The BBC for the 1969 Promenade Concerts

3+1.2+1.3+1.2+1/4.4.2+1.1/xylophone/percussion (2)

Duration: 10'
First performance: London, Royal Albert Hall, 29 July 1969
  BBC Symphony Orchestra, conducted by Alan Bush
  (Broadcast by the BBC on Radio 4 direct from the Royal
  Albert Hall)
Publication: Novello & Co. Ltd. Full score and parts © 1985
Manuscript: British Library, London. MS. Mus. 344: Draft
  short score in pencil (ff. 1-31); full score in ink
  (ff. 32-77). Completed 20 February 1969
Recordings: Kosei Publishing Co. (Japan) KOCD-8012 (2005)
  The Tokyo Kosei Wind Orchestra, conducted by Douglas
  Bostock
Bibliography: *Music and Musicians*, 18 (February 1969), 59
  (A. Orga); *Music Review*, 31, No. 1 (1970), 82-83 (H.
  Raynor); *Musical Opinion*, 92 (September 1969), 621
  (D. Simmons); *Strad*, 80 (September 1969), 225 (Anon.)

OTHER VERSIONS

Arrangement for piano duet
by the composer

Unpublished
Manuscript: British Library, London. MS. Mus. 34 (ff. 78-93)

SONGS OF ASIAN STRUGGLE
Arranged for mixed chorus (SATB) and piano
Words translated by Nancy Bush

(1) 'Polishing the Gun': Song of the Malayan partisans (Andantino moderato)
(2) 'The Joy of Harvest': Song from North Korea (Allegro leggiero)
(3) 'My Country in Captivity': Song of the Huk partisans of the Philippine Islands (Andante affetuoso)
(4) 'The Jacket-Makers' Song': Song from North Vietnam
(5) 'Chinese Students' Song': Song against the Japanese invaders of the 1930s

Duration: 12'
First performance: London, Wigmore Hall, 17 January 1970
  The London Co-operative Youth Choir and Alan Bush
  (piano), conducted by Jonathan Cohen
Publication: Staff and tonic sol-fa notation. WMA © 1970 and 1971
Manuscript: British Library, London. MS. Mus. 423, ff. 23-42: the fourth
  and fifth songs are not included.
  Additional Malayan folk-song arrangements for chorus and piano,
  not included in *Songs of Asian Struggle*, are included in ff. 36-42:
  'Fighting Youth Song', 'Victory Celebration' and 'Red Flag Song'
Bibliography: *Musical Times*, 111 (March 1970), 294-98 (R. Crichton)
Note: Alan Bush had already arranged the Chinese Students' Song for
  mixed chorus (SATB) in 1949 (see arrangements)

THE FREIGHT OF HARVEST (Opus 69)
Song cycle for tenor and piano
Text: Sylvia Townsend Warner

Introduction (Andante moderato)
(1) Country Thought from a Town (Andante, molto quieto)
Interlude I (Andante scorrevole)
(2) The Sailor (Con moto non allegro ma un poco agitato)
(3) The Maiden (Andantino, quasi grazioso)
Interlude II (Allegro moderato)
(4) The Load of Fern (Moderato non largo e scorrevole)

Commissioned by: The 1969 Dartington Summer School
Dedication: "To Joseph Ward"
Duration: 19′
First performance: Dartington, Dartington Hall, 8 August 1969
  Joseph Ward (tenor) and Alan Bush (piano)
First (public) performance: Newcastle upon Tyne, Laing Art
  Gallery, 14 October 1969
  Joseph Ward (tenor) and Alan Bush (piano)
First London performance: London, Wigmore Hall, 17 January 1970
  Joseph Ward (tenor) and Alan Bush (piano)
First broadcast performance: BBC Radio 3, 20 August 1970
  Joseph Ward (tenor) and Alan Bush (piano)
Unpublished
Manuscript: British Library, London. MS. Mus. 425, ff. 26-89: Draft score
  in pencil; score in ink
Bibliography: *Musical Times*, 110 (December 1969), 1275 (A. Phillips);
  Musical Times, 111 (March 1970), 298 (R. Crichton); *Musical
  Times*, 114 (June 1973), 627+ (A. Cross)

SERENADE (Opus 70)
For string quartet
In five movements

(1) Romance (Andante appassionato)
(2) Musette (Allegro vivace)
(3) Air and Variation (a tempo moderato, non largo)
(4) March (Tempo di marcia vivace)
(5) Postlude (Quasi tempo di Romanza)

Commissioned by: The BBC
Dedication: "With admiration and affection to my old friend Ernst
  Hermann Meyer"
Duration: 19′20″
First performance: London, Wigmore Hall, 17 January 1970
  Gabrieli String Quartet
First broadcast performance: BBC Radio 3, 20 August 1970
  Gabrieli String Quartet
Unpublished
Manuscript: British Library, London. MS. Mus. 356, ff. 51-89: Draft score
  in pencil
Bibliography: *Composer*, No. 34 (Winter 1969-1970), 38+ (Anon.)

1970

SONATA [No. 2] in A FLAT ['He Epikoureia Hedone'] (Opus 71)
For piano

Dedication: "In friendship and high esteem to Ronald Stevenson"
Duration: 20'
First performance: Bath, University Theatre, 28 May 1972
  Ronald Stevenson (piano)
First London performance: London, Wigmore Hall, 5 May 1974
  Ronald Stevenson (piano)
First broadcast performance: BBC Radio 3, 30 July 1972
  Ronald Stevenson (piano)
Unpublished
Manuscript: British Library, London. MS. Mus. 356, ff. 90-122:
  Score in ink.
  Also a typewritten list of corrections to the score (f. 91) and
  sketches of the main subject of the sonata (ff. 91-94) which is
  derived from the ancient Greek *First Delphi Hymn to Apollo* as
  transcribed by Isobel Henderson in *The Oxford History of Music*
  (1957), pp. 367-368
Bibliography: *Composer*, No. 44 (Summer 1972), 36 (B. Orr):
  Musical Times, 113 (July 1972), 690 (S. Walsh)

1971

FIFTY FIGHTING YEARS
Music for the film about *Labour Monthly: Journal of Left Unity*
Written by Stanley Forman, Ivor Montagu and Roger Woddis

(1) Introduction (Allegro moderato)
(2) The Land it is the Landlord's (Text: Jones/Tune: Roberts and Bush)
(3) 1919
(4) Immeasurably better
(5) In the 30s
(6) Steps to War
(7) Steps to War (2)
(8) Steps to War (3)
(9) Steps to War (4)
(10) Steps to War (5)
(11) Truth on the March (Text by Randall Swingler)
(12) End titles

0.0.1.0/0.2.2.0/piano/percussion/strings (and chorus)

Duration of film: c.40′
First screening: London, National Film Theatre, 10 June 1973
Unpublished
Manuscript: British Library, London. MS. Mus. 414 (ff. 36): Full score in
  ink and 415 (ff. 157): Copies of the parts in ink
Note: The film tells the story of the *Labour Monthly*, founded by
  Palme Dutt in 1921, and is narrated by Robin Page Arnot and
  Palme Dutt

MEN OF FELLING (Opus 72)
For male voice choir (TTBB) and piano
Text: Nancy Bush

Commissioned by Northern Arts to mark the choir's 50th anniversary and
the Golden Jubilee Choral Champions Concert

Dedication: "To the Felling Male Voice Choir"
Duration: 2′30″
First concert performance: Newcastle upon Tyne, City Hall, 15 October
  1971
  The Felling Male Voice Choir with Kenneth Murray (piano),
  conducted by Norman Williams
Unpublished
Manuscript: British Library, London. MS. Mus. 423, ff. 43-67: Draft score
  in pencil; score in ink
Bibliography: *Newcastle Evening Chronicle*, 16 October 1971, 7
  (B. Bowden); *Newcastle Evening Chronicle* 18 October
  1971, 5 (C. Bowden); *Newcastle Journal*, 16 October 1971,
  6 (B. Cresswell)

80th BIRTHDAY TRIBUTE TO SIR ARTHUR BLISS
For piano
One of a collection of original works (*Greetings to Sir Arthur Bliss*)
presented to Sir Arthur by the Composers' Guild of Great Britain on his
80th birthday (2 August 1971). All in manuscript and bound in a leather
volume. Dated 2 November 1971

The other composers who contributed were:

William Alwyn; Richard Arnell; Malcolm Arnold; Lennox Berkeley; Benjamin Britten; Geoffrey Bush; Francis Chagrin; Arnold Cooke; Adrian Cruft; Stephen Dodgson; Peter Racine Fricker; John Gardner; Joseph Horowitz; Herbert Howells; Elizabeth Maconchy ; Edmund Rubbra; Humphrey Searle; Michael Tippett; Ernest Tomlinson; Graham Whettam; Grace Williams and William Wordsworth

Alan Bush's tribute was a quotation 'From Africa: Symphonic Movement for solo piano and orchestra (Opus 73)' Signed and dated 20 September 1971

Dedication: "To Sir Arthur Bliss"
Unpublished
Manuscript: Lady Bliss

1971-1972

CONCERT OVERTURE FOR AN OCCASION (Opus 74)
For orchestra
Written to celebrate the 150th Anniversary of the Royal Academy of Music

2+1.2+1.2+1.2+1/4.3.3.1/timpani/percussion (2)/celesta/piano/strings
Dedication: "To the student orchestral players of the RAM."
  [printed copy only]
Duration: 8′
First performance: London, Royal Festival Hall, 5 July 1972
  RAM First Orchestra, conducted by Maurice Handford
First broadcast performance: BBC Radio 3, 1 October 1981
  BBC Welsh Symphony Orchestra, conducted by Bryden Thomson
Unpublished
Manuscript: British Library, London. MS. Mus. 346, ff. 1-28: Sketches
  (ff. 2-3) and draft score in pencil

OTHER VERSIONS

Arrangement for wind band
By the composer

First performance: Manchester, Concert Hall, Royal Northern College of
  Music, 22 June 1985
  RNCM Wind Orchestra and Northern Wind Ensemble, conducted

by Clark Rundell
Unpublished
Manuscript: British Library, London. MS. Mus.346, ff. 29-83: Full score in
ink with a typewritten list of corrections to the score and parts,
dated 3 April 1985

1972

AFRICA (Opus 73)
Symphonic movement for solo piano and orchestra

4.4.4.4/4.3.3.1/timpani/percussion(2)/strings
Duration: 25'
First performance: Halle (GDR), 16 October 1972.
  Alan Bush (piano) and the Halle Philharmonic Orchestra
  conducted by Olaf Koch
First British performance: London, St. John's, Smith Square, 20 November
  1976
  Alan Bush (piano) and the London Senior Orchestra, conducted by
  Terence Lovett
First broadcast performance: BBC Radio 3, 1 October 1981
  William Langford (piano) and the BBC Welsh Symphony
  Orchestra conducted by Bryden Thomson
Publication: Peters Edition (Leipzig). Full score © 1974
Manuscript: British Library, London. MS. Mus. 345, ff. 1-52
Bibliography: *World Music*, 15 No. 2 (1973), 67 (Anon.)

OTHER VERSIONS

Arrangement for two pianos
by the composer

Unpublished
Manuscript: British Library, London. MS.Mus.345, ff. 53-105: Score in ink

LIVELY MINUET
For solo piano

First performance: Unable to trace
Unpublished
Manuscript: British Library, London. MS. Mus. 366, ff. 55-56: Score in ink

EARTH HAS GRAIN TO GROW
Part-song for unaccompanied mixed chorus (SATB)
Text: C. Day Lewis

Duration: 2'30"
First performance: Unable to trace
Publication: Novello & Co. Vocal score © 1972
  Printed as a supplement to *Musical Times* (MT 1553) in
  July 1972
Manuscript: British Library, London. MS. Mus. 424, ff. 13-19

THE EARTH AWAKENING (Opus 74) [used for a second time]
Carol for female voices (SSA) and organ (registration provided)
Text: Nancy Bush

Written for The Perse Girls' School (Cambridge) 1972 School Carol
  Service
Duration: 3'
First performance: Cambridge, Parish Church of Great St. Mary's,
  18 December 1972. The Singers
Unpublished
Manuscript: British Library, London. MS. Mus. 424, ff. 20-35: Draft
  score in pencil; score in ink

SONG FOR ANGELA DAVIS (Opus 75)
Part song for unaccompanied mixed chorus (SATB) (or as a unison song)
with piano
Text: Nancy Bush

Duration: 5'
First performance: Sheffield, Wortley Hall, 25 August 1972
  Sheila Searchfield (mezzo-soprano) and the WMA Summer
  School Chorus with Brian Trueman (piano), conducted by
  Alan Bush
Publication: Workers' Music Association. Vocal score © 1972
Manuscript: British Library, London. MS. Mus. 424, ff. 1-12: Dated
March-
  April 1972 and includes a typewritten copy of the text dated
  28 January 1972

CORENTYNE KWE-KWE (Opus 75) [listed as Opus 76]
Toccata for piano

Dedication: "To those men and women of Guyana who faced a
British warship and stood their ground"
Duration: 4'
First performance: Bromsgrove, Shenstone New College, 2 April 1973
Alan Bush (piano) (Bromsgrove Festival)
First London performance: Wigmore Hall, 11 January 1976
William Langford (piano)
Unpublished
Manuscript: British Library, London. MS. Mus. 357, ff. 1-13: Score in ink
Recordings: Altarus Records AIR-CD-9004 (1984/1993)
Peter Jacobs (piano)
Bibliography: *Musical Times*, 114 (June 1973), 627+29 (A. Cross);
The Times, 12 January 1976, 15 (J. Chissell)
Notes: The toccata is based on an African song commemorating the
abolition of slavery in Guyana in 1842. The title is spelt
Corentyne Que-que on the first page of music

1973

THE LIVERPOOL OVERTURE (Opus 76) [listed as Opus 77]
For orchestra

Commissioned by: The Liverpool Trades Council for their 125th
Anniversary celebrations

3.3.3.3/4.3.3.1/timpani/percussion/piano/strings

Duration: 9'
First performance: Liverpool, Philharmonic Hall, 1 May 1973
The Royal Liverpool Philharmonic Orchestra, conducted by
Charles Groves
First broadcast performance: BBC Radio 3, 1 October 1981
The BBC Welsh Symphony Orchestra, conducted by
Bryden Thomson
Unpublished
Manuscript: British Library, London. MS. Mus. 346, ff 84-103:
Full score; ff. 104-135: Draft short score in pencil

FESTIVAL MARCH OF BRITISH YOUTH (Opus 78)
For wind orchestra with guitars, percussion and double bass

3.2.5.2/0.3.3.3/timpani/percussion/guitars (2)/double bass

Duration: 4'
First performance: Berlin, August 1973
Unpublished
Manuscript: British Library, London. MS. Mus. 347, ff. 1-12:
  Full score in ink

1974

SONG DUET (Opus 78, No. 1) **and INTRODUCTION AND
DANCE-DUET** (Opus 78, No. 2)
For clarinet and cello with piano accompaniment
Written for and dedicated to the composer's grandchildren, Niall and
Niav O'Higgins

First performance (Opus 78, No. 1): Cambridge, Technical College,
  ? April 1974. Niall O'Higgins (clarinet) and Niav O'Higgins
  (cello) with Rachel O'Higgins (piano)
First performance (Opus 78, No. 2): Cambridge, Technical College,
  ? April 1975. Niall O'Higgins (clarinet) and Niav O'Higgins
  (cello) with Rachel O'Higgins (piano)
Unpublished
Manuscript: British Library, London. MS. Mus.357, ff. 14-23: Scores
  in ink

LIFE'S SPAN (Opus 77) [listed as Opus 79]
Four songs for mezzo-soprano and piano

(1) A Child Asleep: Text by Nancy Bush (1958) (Molto tranquillo)
(2) Learning to Talk: Text by C. Day Lewis (1961) (Allegro commodo)
(3) The Long Noonday: Text by Nancy Bush (1974) (Andante moderato
     ma appassionata)
(4) Beauty's End is in Sight: Text by C. Day Lewis (1974) (Con moto,
     scorrevole ed espressivo)

Duration: 18'

First performance: (Nos 1 and 2 only, originally written as Opus 48):
        London, Morley College, 19 November 1961
        Anna Pollack (mezzo-soprano) and Alan Bush (piano)

First complete performance: Bromsgrove, Shenstone New College, 2 April
  1973

Katinka Seiner (mezzo-soprano) and Alan Bush (piano)
First London performance: Royal Academy of Music, 23 January 1975
  Suzanne Webborn (soprano) and Roger Steptoe (piano)
First (public) London performance: Wigmore Hall, 11 January 1976
  Laura Sarti (mezzo-soprano) and Alan Bush (piano)
First broadcast performance: BBC Radio 3, 21 Dec 1976
  Laura Sarti (mezzo-soprano) and Alan Bush (piano)
Unpublished except No. 2 (with words in English and Russian)
  Moscow, Sovietskii Kompozitor © 1963
Manuscript: British Library, London. MS. Mus. 426, ff. 1-32: Score in ink;
  draft score in pencil. An earlier title of the third song, *Most
  Constant Grown*, is deleted from the title page (f.18)
Recordings: Musaeus Recordings MZ CD 102 (2000). Phillida Bannister
  (mezzo-soprano) and Richard Black (piano)
Bibliography: *Musical Times*, 114 (June 1973), 627+29 (A. Cross):
  The Times, 12 January 1976, 15 (J. Chissell)

SUITE IN ENGLISH STYLE (Opus 79)[listed as Opus 79A or Opus 79, No. 2]
For string ensemble

(1) Pavan (Maestoso ma non largo)
(2) Cheviot Rant (Allegro vivace)
(3) Soliloquy on a Sailor's Song (Andante tranquillo)
(4) March (Tempo di marcia vivace)

First performance: Unable to trace
Unpublished
Manuscript: British Library, London. MS. Mus.347, ff. 13-23: Score in ink

LETTER GALLIARD (Opus 80)
For piano
Written as a tribute to Shostakovich using the letters DSCH and ABSH, it
was one of 13 short musical compositions to be published as a supplement
to a volume of essays, edited by Grigori Schneerson, published in Moscow
as a 70th-birthday tribute to Shostakovich. In the event, it became a
memorial volume

Duration: 2'30"
First concert performance: London, Wigmore Hall, 11 January 1976
  William Langford (piano)
Publication: Sovietskya Musika. Score © 1974
  Thames Publishing © 2000 (An anthology of British 20th century

piano music. Volume 3)
Manuscript: Whereabouts unknown
Recordings: Altarus Records AIR-CD-9004 (1984/1993)
  Peter Jacobs (piano)
Bibliography: *The Times*, 12 January 1976, 15 (J. Chissell)

1975

SUITE FOR SIX (Opus 81)
For string quartet

Introduction (Moderato)
I Pavan (Maestoso ma non largo)
Interlude I (un pochissimo piu moto)
II Reel (Allegro vivace)
Interlude II
III Andamento (con moto fluente)
Interlude III - Andante appassionata
IV Air (molto cantabile ad appassionato)
Interlude IV - tempo di moto perpetuo
V Moto perpetuo (Presto)
Interlude V - L'istesso tempo
VI Sword Dance (Allegro moderato ma energico)
Postlude (Moderato)

Commissioned by: The BBC
Duration: 26'
First performance: London, St. John's Smith's Square, 15 December 1975
  Chilingirian String Quartet (BBC Lunchtime Concert)
Unpublished
Manuscript: British Library, London. MS. Mus. 357, ff. 24-25: Score in ink
Recordings: Redcliffe Recordings RR 020 (© 2003)
  The Bachmann String Quartet

[DUO] SONATINA (Opus 82)
For descant, treble and tenor recorders (one player) and piano
In three movements

(1) Introduction and Allegro (Allegro moderato/Allegro vivace ma non
     troppo
(2) Andante quasi larghetto (Andante quasi larghetto, molto cantabile)
(3) Vivo (Vivace)

Dedication: "To Ross Winters"
Duration: 15′
First performance: London, Wigmore Hall, 11 January 1976
  Ross Winters (recorder) and Alan Bush (piano)
Publication: Nova Music. Score © 1981
Manuscript: British Library, London. MS. Mus.357, ff. 55-146: Draft score
  in pencil; score in ink
Bibliography: *The Times*, 12 January 1976, 15 (J. Chissell)

1976

COMPASS POINTS (Opus 83)
A Suite for treble, alto, tenor and bass bamboo pipes

(1) North, based on 'Dance to Your Shadow' and 'Islay Reaper's Song
     (Allegro giocoso)
(2) West, based on 'Watching the Wheat' and 'Black Sir Harry' (Andante
     con moto)
(3) East, based on 'The Cruel Sea Captain' (Andante, molto espressivo)
(4) South, based on 'Bedlam City' and 'The Scolding Wife' (Allegretto,
     quasi, leggieramente)

Commissioned by: The Pipers' Guild
Duration: 12′
First performance: Canterbury, St. Augustine's College, 24 August 1976
  The Hopkinson Quartet
Unpublished
Manuscript: British Library, London. MS. Mus.358, ff. 1-17: Score in ink

AFRICA IS MY NAME (Opus 85)
For mezzo-soprano, mixed chorus (SATB) and piano (or orchestra)
Text: Nancy Bush and from African songs

Duration: 10′
First performance Sheffield, Wortley Hall, 20 August 1976
  Annette Gavin (mezzo-soprano), WMA Summer School Chorus
  with Alan Bush (piano)
Unpublished
Manuscript: British Library, London. MS .Mus. 420, ff. 1-19: Vocal score,
  chorus part and solo part in ink

1976-1977

DE PLENOS PODERES ['From Fully Empowered'] (Opus 86)
Song cycle for baritone and piano
Text: Pablo Neruda (in Spanish)

(1) Nada Más (Andante con gravita)
(2) El Perezoso (Allegretto, quasi grazioso)
(3) El Pueblo (Con moto fluente)

Duration: 14'
First performance (Nos 2 and 3 only): London, Wigmore Hall, 11 January
   1976
   Graham Titus (baritone) and Alan Bush (piano)
First complete performance: London, Wigmore Hall, 30 October 1977
   Graham Titus (baritone) and Alan Bush (piano)
First broadcast performance: BBC, Radio 3, 13 July 1981
   Peter Savage (baritone) and Alan Bush (piano)
Unpublished
Manuscript: British Library, London. MS. Mus. 426, ff. 33-72: Score in ink
Bibliography: *Composer*, No. 63 (Spring 1978), 2 (B. Orr), *Music and*
   Musicians, 26 (February 1978), 52-53 (M Barry); *The Times*,
   12 January 1976, 15 (J. Chissell)
Note: Numbers 2 and 3 were originally written as *Two Songs for*
   Baritone and Piano (Opus 80)

1977

TWENTY FOUR PRELUDES (Opus 84)
for piano

(1) Moderato, un poco scorrevole (F sharp Dorian diatonic)
(2) Allegro vivace e leggiero (F sharp Lydian chromatic)
(3) Largo (C sharp Phrygian diatonic)
(4) Andante tranquillo, non largo (C sharp Mixolydian chromatic)

(5) Allegro vivace ma non presto (A flat Aeolian diatonic)
(6) Lento e tranquillo (A flat Pentatonic chromatic)
(7) Allegro leggieramente (E flat Lydian diatonic)
(8) Andante con moto, cantabile ed espressivo (E flat Aeolian chromatic)

(9) Moderato, non largo (B flat Ionian diatonic)
(10) Vivace e leggiero, non presto (B flat Aeolian chromatic)
(11) Larghetto, quasi grazioso (F Phrygian diatonic)
(12) Andante con moto (F Lydian chromatic)

(13) Larghetto, molto espressivo e cantabile (C Dorian chromatic)
(14) Allegro vivace (C Pentatonic diatonic)
(15) Allegro vivace, non presto (G Lydian diatonic)
(16) Andantino, quasi allegretto (G Phrygian chromatic)

(17) Tempestuoso ma non presto (D Aeolian diatonic)
(18) Maestoso, molto largo (D Mixolydian chromatic)
(19) Andantino (A Dorian diatonic)
(20) Allegretto grazioso ed espressivo (A Ionian chromatic)

Vivace leggieramente (E Phrygian diatonic)
Allegro, un poco agitato (E Aeolian chromatic)
Andante, dolce ed espressivo ma sempre cantabile (B Mixolydian diatonic)
Allegro con fuoco (B Dorian chromatic)

Duration: 37'
First performance: London, Wigmore Hall, 30 October 1977
  Alan Bush (piano)
First broadcast performance: BBC Radio 3, 8 April 1979
  Alan Bush (piano)
Publication: Cadenza Music (Newport). Piano score © 2005
Manuscript: British Library, London. MS. Mus. 358, ff. 18-27:
  Score in ink. Nos. 13 and 14 are written in the reverse order
Recordings: Altarus Records AIR-CD-9004 (1984/1993)
  Peter Jacobs (Piano)
Bibliography: *Composer*, No. 63 (Spring 1978), 2 (B. Orr), *Tempo*,
  No. 123 (December 1977), 56 (Anon.)

DERIVED PUBLICATION

The Cheviot Piper
For piano (Grade IV or V)
Based on No. 15 of the 24 Preludes
Manuscript: British Library, London. MS. Mus. 366, ff. 52-54: Score in ink
  The original title, *The Border Piper*, is deleted on the title page

WOMAN'S LIFE (Opus 87)
Song cycle for soprano and piano
Text: Nancy Bush

(1) Prologue (Allegro moderato ma deciso)
(2) Weaving Song (Allegro expressivo)
(3) Factory Day (Allegro agitato)
(4) Epilogue (Andante con moto)

Commissioned by: Woking Music Club
Duration: 14′
First performance: Woking (Surrey), Central Hall, 12 February 1978
  Sylvia Eaves (soprano) and Alan Bush (piano)
First London performance: Wigmore Hall, 28 October 1979
  Patricia Taylor (soprano) and Alan Bush (piano)
First broadcast performance: BBC Radio 3, 15 November 1982
  Dinah Harris (soprano) and Rosemary Barnes (piano)
Unpublished
Manuscript: British Library, London. MS. Mus. 426, ff. 73-91
Recordings: Musaeus Recordings MZ CD 102 (2000)
  Moira Harris (soprano) and Richard Black (piano)
Bibliography: *Musical Times*, 111 (March 1970), 294-98 (R. Crichton)

1978

SONATINA (Opus 88)
For viola and piano
In three movements

1. Introduzione - Allegro moderato (a tempo moderato, non largo) [7′49″]
2. Quasi menuetto (Andantino grazioso ed expressivo) [4′24″]
3. Rondo-Epilogo (Allegro vivace) [6′10″]

Commissioned by: The Viola Research Society for their Congress in
  London, June 1978
Dedication: "To the memory of Cecil Aronowitz" [in printed copy only]
First private performance: London, Royal College of Music, 10 June 1978
  Cecil Aronowitz (viola) and Alan Bush (piano)
  (During the Sixth International Viola Research Society Congress)
First public performance: London, Wigmore Hall, 28 October 1979
  John White (viola) and Alan Bush (piano)

Publication: N. Simrock (London/Hamburg) Score © 1980 (edited by John
  White), viola part from the part used by Cecil Aronowitz at the
  first performance
Manuscript: British Library, London. MS. Mus.358, ff. 73-131: Draft score
  in pencil; score in ink
Recordings: Meridan Records CDE 84458 (2002)
  Adam Summerhayes (viola) and Catherine Summerhayes (piano)
Bibliography: *Music and Musicians*, 26 (August 1978), 36 (T. Homfray)

1979

PRO PACE ET FELICITATE GENERIS HUMANI (Voices of Two
Continents) ['For the Peace and Happiness of Mankind'] (Opus 89)
Rhapsody for cello and piano
Based on melodies from USA: [Earl Robinson 'The Ballad of Joe Hill']
Great Britain: [Carl Dallas 'The Family of Man'] and the USSR:
[Borodin – 'Prince Igor' and a song by Dunayevsky]

Dedication: "To the British-Bulgarian Friendship Society" [in printed
  copy only]
Duration: 8'
First performance: London, Camden Town Hall, 18 May 1979
  Cathy Giles (cello) and Alan Bush (piano)
Unpublished
Manuscript: British Library, London. MS. Mus.359, ff. 1-21: Score and
  cello part in ink

1980

VOICES FROM FOUR CONTINENTS (Opus 91)
Rondo for clarinet, cello and piano

(1)   Africa: Mozambique – *Hymn of the Revolution* (Dombo)
(2)   Asia: Vietnam – *Song of Liberation* (Văn Chung)
(3)   Americas: Chile – '*Manifiesto*' (Victor Jara)
(4)   Europe: USSR – *Steppe Cavalry* (Lev Knipper)

Duration: 6'
First performance: London, Camden Town Hall, 10 May 1980
  Rory Allam (clarinet), Cathy Giles (cello) and Alan Bush
  (piano) (British Soviet Friendship Society, 2nd International Festival)
Unpublished

Manuscript: British Library, London. MS. Mus. 359, ff. 22-38: Score and parts in ink

TWO SHAKESPEARE SONNETS (Opus 92)
For baritone and chamber orchestra
Text: William Shakespeare

Introduction (Andantino scorrevole)
Sonnet No. 18: 'Shall I Compare Thee to a Summer's Day?'
  (Con moto moderato, non largo)
Sonnet No. 60: 'Like as the Waves Make Towards the Pebbled Shore'
  (Andantino, un poco agitato)

1.1.1.0/2.0.4.0/timpani/percussion/piano/strings

Dedication: "To Nancy Bush" [with a note of presentation to her on the 50th anniversary of their wedding, 31 March 1981]
Duration: 15′
First public performance: London, Royal Albert Hall, 5 August 1981. Graham Titus (baritone) and the BBC Welsh Symphony Orchestra, conducted by Bryden Thomson
Unpublished
Manuscript: British Library, London. MS. Mus. 420, ff. 20-71: Full score in ink. Dated 16 September 1980
Bibliography: *Musical Times*, 122 (October 1981), 688 (B. Millington)

MEDITATION AND SCHERZO (Opus 93, No 2)
For double bass and piano

Duration: Meditation (Allegro molto) [5′00″]
  Scherzo (Allegro vivace) [4′00″]
First performance: Meditation (on the ballad 'Geordie' and originally designated as Opus 62) only – Bracknell (Berkshire), South Hill Park Arts Centre, 25 April 1980
  Roger Dean (double bass) and Alan Bush (piano)
First complete performance: London, British Music Information Centre, 11 December 1980
  Roger Dean (double bass) and Alan Bush (piano)
Publication: Yorke Edition. Score © 1982
Manuscript: British Library, London. MS. Mus. 355, ff. 88-97 and 359, ff. 39-54: Score and double bass part in ink
Bibliography: *Notes*, 42 No. 1 (1985), 156-57 (Anon.)

CONCERTINO (Opus 94)
For two violins and piano

1. Introduction and Allegro Energico
2. Fughetta
3. Autumn Song
4. Cadenza, leading to Dance

Dedication: "To Hazel and Maureen Smith"
Duration: 29′
First performance: Aldeburgh, Jubilee Hall, 18 June 1981
  Hazel Smith and Maureen Smith (violins) with Alan Bush
  (piano)
First broadcast performance: BBC Radio 3, 19 November 1982.
  Hazel Smith and Maureen Smith (violins) with Alan Bush
  (piano)
Unpublished
Manuscript: British Library, London. MS. Mus. 359, ff. 55-140: Score and
  violin parts in ink. [Begun 1980], completed 14 February 1981

1980-1983

SIX SHORT PIECES (Opus 99)
For piano

Originally written for Anna Ambrose

(1) Invention for Two Voices (Andantino) [1′02″]
(2) Evening Lyric (Larghetto) [1′24″]
(3) Tyneside Reel (Allegro vivace, non presto) [0′ 58″]
(4) Ceremonial (Largo, non lento) [1′25″]
(5) Song (Moderato con moto) [1′43″]
(6) Rondino (Allegro vivace) [2′25″]

First performance: Unable to trace
First (concert) performance: London, Queen Elizabeth Hall, 10
  January 1986
  Alan Bush (piano)
Published: Goodmusic Publishing (including Roberton Publications)
  Score © 1988 (Roberton Publications No. 5560)
Manuscript: British Library, London. MS. Mus.360, ff. 15-36:
  Score in ink

Recordings: Claudio Records CB5151-2 (recorded and issued in 1984, re-issued in 2002). Alan Bush (piano)
Bibliography: *Tempo*, No. 153 (June 1985), 39-40 (C. MacDonald)

1981-1982

SCOTS JIGGANSPIEL (Opus 95)
For piano

Based on 'Sweet Molly', 'Duke of Perth', 'Tullochgorum', 'Strathspern', 'Marquis of Huntley's Farewell' and 'Stumpie' published in *The Select Melodies of Scotland*, Edinburgh, 1822

Dedication: "Dedicated in warm affection to Ronald Stevenson"
First performance: Unable to trace
Unpublished
Manuscript: British Library, London. MS. Mus.360, ff. 1-11: Photocopy of the autograph manuscript, with photocopied and autograph correction slips added

SONG AND DANCE (Opus 96)
For junior string orchestra
Text for 'Song' developed from the Scottish folk-song to which Robert Burns wrote the poem 'The Collier Bonnie Lassie'
Dance: Based on the folksongs 'Dance to Your Shadow' and 'The Islay Reaper's Song'

First performance: Unable to trace
Unpublished
Manuscript: British Library, London. MS. Mus.347, ff. 24-40: Score in ink; parts in ink for the *Dance* only

1982-1983

SYMPHONY No. 4 (LASCAUX) (Opus 98)
For orchestra

(1) The Wild (Molto moderato e quieto) [originally entitled 'Lascaux Impression']
(2) The Children (Allegro vivace)
(3) Ice Age Remembered (Molto largo)

(4) Mankind Emergent (Allegretto scorrevole) [originally entitled 'Man
     Emergent']

4.3.3.3/2.2.3.1/timpani/percussion/harp/piano/strings

Duration: 40′
First performance: Manchester, BBC Studios, 15 March 1986
  The BBC Philharmonic Orchestra, conducted by Edward Downes
First broadcast performance: BBC Radio 3, 25 March 1986.
  The BBC Philharmonic Orchestra, conducted by Edward Downes
Unpublished
Manuscript: British Library, London. MS. Mus. 348 (ff. 132): Full
  score in ink

1983

A SONG FROM THE NORTH (Opus 97)
For piano
Based on a calling-on song used by the sword-dancers of Earsdon in
Northumberland

Dedication: "To Thomas Pitfield from Alan Bush, 17 February 1983"
First performance: Altringham, All Saints Church (New Street), 6 May 1983
  Stephen Reynolds (piano)
Publication: Forsyth Ltd. (Manchester). Score © 1983
  ('A Birthday Album for Thomas Pitfield')
Manuscript: British Library, London. MS. Mus. 360, ff. 12-14: Score in ink

SUMMER FIELDS AND HEDGEROWS (Opus 100)
Two Impressions for clarinet and piano

Dedication: "To Nancy Bush"
First performance: Unable to trace
Unpublished
Manuscript: British Library, London. MS. Mus.360, ff. 37-67: Score and
  clarinet part in ink. Dated June-July 1983

1984

OCTET (Opus 105)
For flute, clarinet, horn, string quartet and piano
in five movements

Moderato, non largo
Allegro vivace
Andante con moto
Allegro leggieramente
Moderato – Allegro moderato

Duration: 16'30"
First performance: Unable to trace
Unpublished
Manuscript: British Library, London. MS. Mus. 361(ff. 157): Draft score in
   pencil; score and parts in ink. Dated 14 November 1984

THREE EASY FIVE BEAT FIRST YEAR PIECES (Opus 114)
For piano

1.   With a steadily flowing crotchet
2.   With a flowing quaver
3.   With a fairly fast flowing crotchet

Duration: c.6'
First performance: Unable to trace
Publication: Bardic Edition, Cleveland (Ohio). Score © 1987
Manuscript: British Library, London. MS. Mus. 364, ff. 35-38: Score in ink

1984-1985

THE EARTH IN SHADOW (Opus 102)
For mixed chorus (SATB) and orchestra
Text: Nancy Bush

2+1.2+1.2+1.2/4.3.2.0/timpani/percussion(2)/piano/strings

Dedication: "To Nancy Bush"
Duration: c.12'
First performance: London, Great Hall (Goldsmiths College), 27
   September 1986
   Goldsmiths' College Student Orchestra and Choir, conducted by
   Roger Wibberley
Publication: Goodmusic Publishing (including Roberton Publications)
   Vocal score © 2005 (Roberton Publications No. 3106)
Manuscript: British Library, London. MS. Mus. 421 (ff. 10): Full and
   vocal score in ink

QUINTET FOR PIANO AND STRINGS (Opus 104)
in four movements

1. Introduction and Allegro (Moderato con gravita)
2. Meditation (Andante quieto ma non largo)
3. Scherzo allegro viva, non presto)
4. Epilogue (Grave)

First performance: Birmingham, BBC Studios, 12 December 1985
  Medici Quartet and John Bingham (piano)
  (Broadcast by the BBC on Radio 3)
First London performance: Queen Elizabeth Hall, 10 January 1986
  Medici Quartet and John Bingham (piano)
Unpublished
Manuscript: British Library, London. MS. Mus. 360, ff. 68-119: Score in
  ink
Bibliography: *Composer*, No. 87 (Spring 1986), 33 (C. De Souza);
  Musical Times, 127 (April 1986), 223 (A. Cross)

1985

TURKISH WORKERS' MARCHING SONG (Opus 101)
For unison chorus, flute, clarinet, trumpet, tenor trombone, piano,
timpani (optional) and percussion
Text: Anonymous

First performance: Unable to trace
Unpublished
Manuscript: British Library, London. MS. Mus.420, ff. 72-75: Full score in
  ink. Text in Turkish

CANZONA (Opus 106)
For flute, clarinet, violin, cello and piano

Dedication: "To Nancy Bush"
Duration: 12′
First performance: Unable to trace
Unpublished
Manuscript: British Library, London. MS. Mus. 362, ff. 103: Draft score in
  pencil; score and parts in ink

MEDITATION FOR ORCHESTRA IN MEMORY OF ANNA AMBROSE
(Opus 107)

2+1.2+1.2.2/4.3.2+1.1/percussion(2)/piano/harp/strings

Duration: 11′
First performance: Unable to trace
Unpublished
Manuscript: British Library, London. MS. Mus. 349, ff. 1-48: Full score in ink

OTHER VERSIONS

Arrangement for piano
by the composer

Unpublished [a note on the manuscript reveals that it was not intended for performance]

MANDELA SPEAKING (Opus 110)
For baritone solo and mixed chorus (SATB) with orchestra or piano
Text: Nelson Mandela

2.2.2.2/4.0.0.0/percussion/piano/strings
First performance: Sheffield, Wortley Hall, August 1986
  WMA choir and orchestra with Alan Bush (piano)
Unpublished
Manuscript: British Library, London. MS. Mus. 420, ff. 76-114: Sketches, vocal and full scores in ink. Texts in English, Xhosa and Zulu
Bibliography: *Composer*, No. 89 (Winter 1986), 28 (C. De Souza)

1986

TWO PRELUDES AND FUGUES (Opus 108)
For violin and piano

Prelude and Fugue in Dorian Mode on G (Opus 108/1) [4′58″]
Interlude [0′35″]
Prelude and Fugue in Mixolydian Mode on D (Opus 108/2) [4′18″]

First performance: Unable to trace
Unpublished

Manuscript: British Library, London. MS. Mus. 363, ff. 1-22: Score of violin part in ink
Recordings: Meridian Records CDE 84481 (2004)
  Adam Summerhayes (violin) and Catherine Summerhayes (piano)

DISTANT FIELDS (Opus 109) [listed as Opus 109a or 109, No. 1]
For piano

First performance: Unable to trace
Unpublished
Manuscript: British Library, London. MS. Mus.363, ff. 23-27: Draft score in pencil

SONG POEM [A tempo moderato ma energico] **and SONG DANCE** [Allegro vivo ma non presto] (Opus 109) [listed Opus 109, No. 2]
For string orchestra and piano

Dedication: "To John Amis"
Duration: 14′
First performance: Unable to trace
Unpublished
Manuscript: British Library, London. MS. Mus.349, ff. 49-58: Full score in ink

SERENADE AND DUET (Opus 111)
For violin and piano

Serenade (Moderato espressivo) [6′41″]
Duet (Allegretto vivace ma non presto) [6′31″]

Dedication: "To Nancy, my life's companion for more than fifty years"

First performance: Unable to trace
Publication: Stainer & Bell Ltd. Score © 1988 [a note on the manuscript reveals that it was sent to the printers on 23 April 1987]
Manuscript: British Library, London. MS. Mus. 363, ff. 28-78: Draft score in pencil; score and violin part in ink. Dated 1-16 January 1986 'Definitive score' and part also in ink
Recordings: Meridian Records CDE 84481 (2004)
  Adam Summerhayes (violin) and Catherine Summerhayes (piano)

SONATA No. 3 in G (Mixolydian) FOR PIANO (Opus 113)
in four movements

1. Moderato serioso
2. Andante espressivo
3. Allegro vivo ma non troppo
4. Allegro energico

Duration: 16′
First performance: London, British Music Information Centre (Stratford
    Place), 28 October 1986
    Leslie Howard (piano)
Unpublished
Manuscript: British Library, London. MS. Mus. 364, ff. 1-34: Sketches and
    drafts in pencil and ink. Final version in ink
Bibliography: *Composer*, No. 90 (Spring 1987), 30 (S. McGinnis); *Tempo*,
    No. 159 (December 1986), 50

[THREE] PIECES 'FOR NANCY' (Opus 115)
For piano

1. Allegro moderato, sempre cantabile
2. Larghetto ma espressivo molto non troppo largo, quasi recitativo
3. Cantabile ed espressivo

Dedication: "To Nancy"
First performance: Unable to trace
Unpublished
Manuscript: British Library, London. MS.Mus.364, ff. 39-69: Draft in ink
    and pencil. Score in ink. A 'Third Piece for my dear Nancy' in ink.
    Numbered 'Opus 120' on the first page of music; corrected to
    'Opus 115' on the title page

PRELUDE [Allegro moderato] **AND CONCERT PIECE** [Con moto
moderato ma energico] (Opus 116)
For organ

Dedication: "To Robert Crowley"
Duration: 16′30″
First performance: Radlett, Christchurch Parish Church, ? December
    1986. Robert Crowley (organ)
Unpublished

Manuscript: British Library, London. MS. Mus. 364, ff. 70-95: Score in ink with a *photocopy* of a revised version of the last page of the *Concert Piece*
Another manuscript of the Prelude was sold at Sotheby's on 21 May 2004, Lot 40: Now in private hands
Recordings: Pipework Records SCS 655 (2000)
  Robert Crowley (organ)
  (Recorded in St. Mary's Parish Church, Hitchin)

SUITE (Opus 117)
For organ
In four movements

1. Dorian on E (Allegro moderato) [2'20"]
2. Phrygian on A (Andantino) [4'45"]
3. Aeolian on C (Largo) [2'50"]
4. Mixolydian on D [4'34"]

Dedication: "To Robert Crowley"
First performance: Unable to trace
Unpublished
Manuscript: In private hands. Sold at Sotheby's on 21 May 2004, Lot 40
Recordings: Pipework Records SCS 655 (2000)
  Robert Crowley (organ)
  (Recorded in St. Mary's Parish Church, Hitchin)

SONG [Andante espressivo] **AND DANCE** (Opus 117) [listed as Opus 117A]
For violin and piano

Duration: Unable to trace
First performance: Unable to trace
Unpublished
Manuscript: British Library, London. MS. Mus. 364, ff. 96-104: Score in ink
Recordings: Meridian Records CDE 84481 (© 2004)
  Adam Summerhayes (violin) and Catherine Summerhayes (piano)

1987

SEPTET (Opus 118) [listed as Opus 118, No. 2]
For flute, oboe, clarinet, bassoon and strings (1.0.1.1)
In five movements

1. Allegro moderato
2. Largamente ma non troppo lento
3. Recitative and Trio
4. Presto
5. Allegro moderato

First performance: Unable to trace
Unpublished
Manuscript: British Library, London. MS. Mus. 365, ff. 33-92: Score and
  parts in ink

TWO ETUDES (Opus 118) [listed as Opus 118A]
For piano

1. Flowing, not very rapid
2. Allegro, non presto

First performance: Unable to trace
Unpublished
Manuscript: British Library, London. MS. Mus. 365, ff. 8-18: Score in ink

SONATA No. 4 in FOR PIANO (Opus 119)

Moderato, molto espressivo-Allegro energico-grazioso-a tempo moderato,
non veloce-Andante appassionato-a tempo tranquillo, piu lento-Andante
appassionato-a tempo tranquillo-a tempo piano-grazioso-un poco cantabile

Dedication: "Dedicated in friendship and high esteem to Ronald
  Stevenson"
First performance: London, British Music Information Centre (Stratford
  Place), ? 1991
  Peter Jacobs (piano)
Unpublished
Manuscript: Whereabouts unknown

SONATA FOR CELLO and PIANO (Opus 120)
In four movements

1. Allegro energico [3′28″]
2. Larghetto, molto espressivo [8′28″]
3. A tempo moderato, sempre cantibile [3′06″]
4. Allegro non troppo ma molto energico [2′15″]

First performance: Unable to trace
Unpublished
Manuscript: British Library, London. MS. Mus. 366, ff. 23-43: Score in ink
Recordings: Dutton CDLX 7130 (2002)
  D. Kennedy (cello) and P. Fowke (piano)

A HEART'S EXPRESSION (Opus 121) [listed as Opus 121, No. 1]
For piano

Dedication: "To Nancy Bush"
First performance: Unable to trace
Unpublished
Manuscript: British Library, London. MS. Mus. 366, ff. 44-51: Score in
  ink. Lacking the second movement

SONATA FOR ORGAN (Opus 118)
In five movements

1. Moderato con moto [4'20"]
2. Theme and Variations (un poco piu animato) [3'21"]
3. Fugue (Allegro moderato) [2'35"]
4. Adagio [3'27"]
5. Allegro vivace [3'27"]

Dedication: "To Robert Crowley"
First performance: Unable to trace
Unpublished
Manuscript: In private hands. Sold at Sotheby's on 21 May 2004, Lot 40
Recordings: Pipework records SCS 655 (© 2000)
  Robert Crowley (organ)
  (Recorded in St. Mary's Parish Church, Hitchin)

TWO PRELUDES AND FUGUES (Opus 118) [corrected on the title page but
not elsewhere to 'Opus 121'; listed as Opus 123 or Opus 121, No. 2]
For piano

Prelude and Fugue in Dorian Mode on G (Con moto moderato, ma deciso
  energico)
Interlude (Moderato, quasi largo)
Prelude and Fugue in Mixolydian Mode on D (Moderato, quasi allegro)

Duration: 12'

First performance: Unable to trace
Unpublished
Manuscript: British Library, London. MS. Mus. 365, ff. 19-32

THE SIX MODES (Opus 119) [corrected on the title page but not elsewhere to 'Opus 122'; listed as Opus 119A or 122]
For piano duet

Mixolydian Mode on D (Con moto moderato)
Dorian Mode on Eb (Andante cantabile)
Phrygian Mode on C (Moderato energico)
Lydian Mode on B (Allegro moderato quasi energico)
Aeolian Mode on E (Gravamente non lentamente)
Ionian Mode on A (Allegro energico)

First performance: Unable to trace
Unpublished
Manuscript: British Library, London. MS. Mus. 366, ff. 1-22: Score in ink

1988

TWO PIECES FOR PIANO (Opus 118) [listed as Opus 124 or Opus 118, No. 1]

(1) Spring Woodland (Moderato)
(2) Summer Garden (Moderato serioso)

First performance: Unable to trace
Unpublished
Manuscript: British Library, London. MS. Mus. 365, ff. 93-99: Score in ink

SUMMER VALLEY (Opus 125)
For cello and piano

Duration: 3'30"
First performance: St. Albans (Herts), Maltings Arts Centre, 27 February 2002.
  Joseph Spooner (cello) and Catherine Summerhayes (piano)
Unpublished

Manuscript: British Library, London. MS. Mus. 366, ff. 60-66: Score and
  cello part in blue ink
Recordings: Meridian Records CDE 84458 (2002)
  Joseph Spooner (cello) and Catherine Summerhayes (piano)

1991-1992

SONATA [No. 5] FOR PIANO
in five movements

Dedication: "To the memory of my dearly beloved wife, Nancy"
Manuscript: British Library, London. MS. Mus. 365, ff. 1-7: In ink
Incomplete: Only the start of the first movement and the
end of the final (fifth) movement exist. Also a second copy
of the first two page (f. 7)

UNDATED WORKS

A Bridge to the Right
Song for mixed chorus
Unpublished

For the People's Use
Song for mixed chorus
Text: Randall Swingler

It's up to us
Song for unison voices and piano with audience participation
Text: Etta Frennell
Unpublished
Manuscript: British Library, London. MS. Mus. 424, ff. 36-37

Learning to talk
Song for mixed chorus
Unpublished

Once is Enough
Song for mixed chorus
Unpublished

Peace and Prosperity
A satirical review with text by Randall Swingler
Unpublished

(The) People's Day
Song for mixed chorus
Text: Randall Swingler

Round the World
For cello and piano
Unpublished
Manuscript: Royal Academy of Music, London. MS 1743
Note: It contains movements with the titles "England", "France" and "China"

Song of the Age
Song for female voices (SSA) and piano
Text: Randall Swingler
Unpublished
Manuscript: British Library, London. MS.Mus.424, ff. 53-66

Song of the Engineers
Song for solo voice, unison chorus and piano
Text: Rhoda Fraser
Unpublished
Manuscript: British Library, London. MS. Mus. 424, ff. 71-72

Till Right Be Done
Song for mixed chorus

Workmates, We Must Fight and Strive
Song for mixed chorus
Text: Randall Swingler
Unpublished
Note: This work is mentioned by Ernst Meyer in his article on The
   Choral Works in the WMA 50th birthday symposium (1950)

You Have Betrayed Our Friends
Song for mixed chorus
Text: Unable to trace
Unpublished
Note: This work is also mentioned by Ernst Meyer in his article on The
   Choral Works in the WMA 50th birthday symposium (1950)

Arrangements of works
by
other composers

African National Congress Anthem (N'kosi Sikeleki Afrike)
Arranged for mixed chorus (SATB) and piano
Dated 11 September 1982

Agincourt Song (c.1415)
Arranged for 3-part mixed chorus (S/A + TB)
Publication: WMA © 1945 (*English Classical Song Series No 2*)

ALEXANDROV, A.V.

Patriotic Song
Arranged for mixed chorus (SATB) and orchestra
English text: J. Alford
First performance: London, Royal Albert Hall, 27 June 1943
  Combined choirs with the London Philharmonic Orchestra,
  conducted by David Ellenberg

Asikatali (South African song)
Arranged for mixed chorus (SATB) and piano
Publication: WMA © 1965 (*From the Five Continents*)

Austrian Workers' Song
Arranged for mixed chorus (SATB) and band
First performance: London, Wembley Stadium, 2 July 1938
  Combined choirs and band, conducted by Alan Bush
Manuscript: British Library, MS. Mus. 399, ff. 58-61

BACH, J.S.

Chorale-Prelude 'Kyrie, Gott, heiliger Geist' (BWV 671)
Arranged for string orchestra (transposed from Bb to C major)
First performance: Cambridge, Arts Theatre, 9 November 1941
  The London String Orchestra, conducted by Alan Bush
First London performance: Aeolian Hall, 6 December 1941.
  The London String Orchestra, conducted by Alan Bush
Manuscript: British Library, MS. Mus. 427, ff. 48-50

Concerto in D minor for two violins and orchestra (BWV 1043)
Arranged for two violins and piano [1980]
Manuscript: British Library, MS. Mus. 428, ff.1-13

Contrapuncti I, V, IX and XI (*Art of Fugue*) (BWV 1080)
Arranged for string orchestra
First performance: London, Wigmore Hall, 25 March 1939
  The London String Orchestra, conducted by Alan Bush
Bibliography: *The Times*, 27 March 1939,19 (Anon.)

Contrapuncti I, IV and XI (*Art of Fugue*) (BWV 1080)
Arranged for string orchestra
First performance: London, Aeolian Hall, 2 November 1941
  The London String Orchestra, conducted by Alan Bush
Bibliography: *The Times*, 4 November 1941, 6 (Anon.)

Fuga super 'Jesus Christus, unser Heiland' (BWV 689)
Arranged for string orchestra (transposed from F to G minor)
First performance: Cambridge, Arts Theatre, 9 November 1941
  The London String Orchestra, conducted by Alan Bush
First London performance: Aeolian Hall, 6 December 1941.
  The London String Orchestra, conducted by Alan Bush
Manuscript: British Library, MS. Mus. 427, ff. 44-45

Invention in F minor (BWV 795)
Arranged for string orchestra
Manuscript: British Library, MS. Mus. 427, ff. 42-43

Prelude from the English Suite No.3 in G minor (BWV 808)
Arranged for string orchestra (transposed to E minor)
Manuscript: British Library, MS. Mus. 427, ff. 36-41

LIKE RIVERS FLOWING
Part song for unaccompanied mixed voices (SSATB)
Text: Nancy Bush

Dedication: "To the people of Llangollen and all who sing there"
  [originally "For the WMA Singers, Welsh Festival]
Duration: 2'50"
First performance: Unable to trace
Publication: Joseph Williams Ltd. Vocal score © 1957
Manuscript: British Library, London. MS. Mus. 422, ff. 61-68: dated
  13 March 1957; sketches in Deposit 2005/32

Two Songs for mezzo-soprano and piano Op. 48, see *Life's Span* Opus 77

1957-1958

TWO BALLADS OF THE SEA (Opus 50)
For piano

(1) The Cruel Sea Captain (Assai mosso, nello stile di un canto populare)
(2) [2'30"]
(3) Reuben Ranzo (Allegro vivace) [4'30"]

Dedication: "Dedicated in friendship and admiration to John Ireland"
First performance: London, Leighton House (Holland Park Road), 16
  December 1960
  Alasdair Graham (piano) (A 60th birthday concert)
Publication: J. Williams Ltd. Score © 1961
Manuscript: British Library, London. MS. Mus.353, ff. 88-10: Scores in ink

1958

NICHT DEN TOD AUS DER FERNE!
For baritone, unison chorus and instrumental ensemble
Text: Armin Müller

Instrumentation: Clarinet, trumpet, percussion and piano
Duration: 2'30"
First performance: Weimar 1958. Unable to trace further details
Unpublished
Manuscript: British Library, London MS. Mus 417, ff. 26-27: Vocal score
  in blue ink

Allegro energico ma non troppo [Theme and 13 variations]
Nocturne (Molto moderato)
Finale (Allegro energico)

2+1.2.2.2/4.2.3.1/timpani/percussion(2)/strings
"Dedicated in friendship and admiration to Sir Thomas Armstrong"
Duration: 21'
First performance: Cheltenham, Town Hall, 7 July 1965
  David Wilde (piano) with the BBC Northern and Midland Light
  Orchestras, conducted by Meredith Davies
Unpublished
Manuscript: British Library, London. MS. Mus. 342, ff. 36: Full score
  in ink; sketch in Deposit 2005/32
Bibliography: *Music and Musicians*, 14 (September 1965), 28
  (B. Jacobson); *Musical Opinion*, 88 (September 1965), 723
  (E.M. Webster); *Musical Times*, 106 (September 1965), 686
  (R. Henderson); *The Times*, 8 July 1965, 17 (Anon.)

OTHER VERSIONS

Arrangement for two pianos
The orchestral part arranged for a second piano by David Lyon

Publication: Novello & Co. Score © 1973

TWO MELODIES (Opus 47)
For viola and piano accompaniment

(1) Song-Melody (Andante elegiaco) [3'57"]
(2) Dance-Melody [2'22"]

Dedication: "In admiration and affection to Lionel Tertis" [only in the
  printed copy]
First performance: BBC, Home Service, 8 January 1959
  Bernard Shore (viola) and Clifton Halliwell (piano)
Publication: Joseph Williams Ltd. Score and parts © 1959
Manuscript: British Library, London. MS. Mus.353, ff. 74-87: Score ink
  sketch in Deposit 2005/32
Recordings: Meridian Records CDE 84458 (2002)
  Adam Summerhayes (viola) and Catherine Summerhayes (piano)

Ricercare a 6 voci (*The Musical Offering*) (BWV 1079)
Arranged for string orchestra (transposed from C to E minor)
First performance: London, Wigmore Hall, 30 January 1939
  The London String Orchestra, conducted by Alan Bush
Manuscript: British Library, MS. Mus. 427, ff. 51-57
Bibliography: *Musical Times,* 80 (March 1939), 222-3 (MMS)

(The) Beaux of the City of London

Arranged for mixed chorus (SATB) and band
First performance: London, Wembley Stadium, 2 July 1938
  Combined choirs and band, conducted by Alan Bush
Manuscript: British Library, MS. Mus. 398, ff. 5-8

BEETHOVEN, L van

Grosse Fuge
Arranged for string orchestra
First performance: London, Wigmore Hall, 18 February 1940
  The London String Orchestra, conducted by Alan Bush
Bibliography: *Musical Times*, 81 (March 1940), 132 (W. McNaught);
  The Times, 20 February 1940,6 (Anon.)

Largo (Piano Sonata, Opus 10, No.3)
Arranged for brass band [1934]
Manuscript: British Library, MS. Mus. 427, ff..109-124

Scherzo (Symphony No. 3, Opus 55)
Arranged for brass band [1934]
Manuscript: British Library, MS. Mus. 427, ff. 125-148

Waltzes: Numbers 1, 3 and 5 (6 *Laendrische Taenze*)
Arranged for string orchestra
First performance: London, Wigmore Hall, 30 January 1939
  The London String Orchestra, conducted by Alan Bush
Bibliography: *Musical Times*, 80 (March 1939), 222-3 (MMS)

Billy Boy

Arranged for soprano and baritone soli, mixed chorus (SAB) and piano
Publication: J. Williams Ltd. © 1955 (*20 Sing for Pleasure Songs*)

Blackbirds and Thrushes
Arranged for mixed chorus (SAB) and piano
First performance: Southend, SE Essex Technical College, 20 September
  1952. WMA Singers, conducted by Alan Bush
Publication: J. Williams Ltd. © 1955 (*20 Sing for Pleasure Songs*)

Blow Ye Winds
Arranged for bass solo, mixed chorus (SAB) and piano
Publication: J. Williams Ltd. © 1955 (*20 Sing for Pleasure Songs*)

Bonny Green Garters
Arranged for mixed choir (SATB) and band
First performance: London, Wembley Stadium, 2 July 1938
  Combined choirs and band, conducted by Alan Bush
Manuscript: British Library, MS. Mus. 398, ff. 3-4

BORODIN, A.

Mazurka
Arranged for piano duet
Publication: WMA. Score [© 1948]

BOYCE, W.

Symphony No. 8 in D minor
Arranged for string orchestra and harpsichord (with flutes and oboes)
First performance: London, Aeolian Hall, 28 October 1939
  The London String Orchestra, conducted by Alan Bush
First broadcast performance (first movement only): London, BBC
  Pacific Service, 10 August 1941. LSO conducted by Alan Bush

Brigg Fair
Arranged for mixed chorus (SAB) and piano
Publication: J. Williams Ltd. © 1955 (*20 Sing for Pleasure Songs*)

BURKHARD, W.

Toccata
Arranged for string orchestra
First performance: London, Wigmore Hall, 18 February 1940
  The London String Orchestra, conducted by Alan Bush
Bibliography: *Musical Times*, 81 (March 1940), 132 (W. McNaught);
  The Times, 20 February 1940, 6 (Anon.)

(The) Careful Carter
Arranged for mixed chorus (SAB) and piano
Publication: J. Williams Ltd. © 1955 (*20 Sing for Pleasure Songs*)

Carmagnole
French folksong arranged for mixed chorus (SATB)
First performance: London, King George's Hall (WC2), 16 June 1949
  The WMA Singers, conducted by Alan Bush

Chinese Students' Song
Arranged for mixed chorus (SATB)
First performance: London, King George's Hall (WC2), 16 June 1949
  The WMA Singers, conducted by Alan Bush

COLEMAN, C.

Fantasia No. 5
Arranged for string orchestra
First performance: London, Aeolian Hall, 28 October 1939
  The London String Orchestra, conducted by Alan Bush
Bibliography: *Musical Times*, 80 (November 1939), 775-6 (WG)

(The) Collier's Rant
Arranged for baritone solo, mixed chorus (SAB) and piano
First performance: Southend, SE Essex Technical College, 20 September
  1952. WMA Singers, conducted by Alan Bush
Publication: J. Williams Ltd. © 1955 (*20 Sing for Pleasure Songs*)

Come Lasses and Lads
Arranged for mixed chorus (SATB) and band
First performance: London, Wembley Stadium, 2 July 1938
  Combined choirs and band, conducted by Alan Bush
Manuscript: British Library, MS. Mus. 398, ff. 14-16

Comrade dear, come home: Song of the Partisans
Arranged for mixed voices (SATB)
First performance: London, Fyvie Hall, 12 December 1944
  The WMA Singers, conducted by Alan Bush

CORELLI, A.

Concerto Grosso No. 5
Arranged for string orchestra
First performance: London, Wigmore Hall, 15 June 1941
  The London String Orchestra, conducted by Alan Bush
First broadcast performance: BBC Home Service, 20 December 1942
  The London String Orchestra, conducted by Alan Bush
Bibliography: *The Times*, 17 June 1941, 6 (Anon.)

Czech National Anthem

(i) Kde Domov Muji and (ii) Nad Tatrou sä Blyska
Arranged for mixed chorus (SATB) and military band
First performance: London, Wembley Stadium, 2 July 1938
  Combined choirs and band, conducted by Alan Bush
Manuscript: British Library, MS. Mus. 399, ff. 50-53

DALLAS, K.

The Family of Man (Europe)
Arranged for mixed chorus (SATB) and piano
Publication: WMA © 1965 (*From the Five Continents*)

DEGEYTER, P.

The International
(1) Arranged for mixed chorus (SATB)
Publication: The Left Song Book (Gollancz © 1938)
(2) Arranged for mixed chorus (SATB), 2 pianos, brass and percussion
  [*circa* 1940]
Manuscript: British Library, MS. Mus. 416, ff. 28-35
(3) Arranged by Bush and arranged for brass band by T.C. Brown
Publication: Hawkes & Son © 1942 (for the WMA)
(4) Arranged for mixed chorus (SATB) and military band [1948]
First performance: London, Royal Albert Hall, 30 March 1948
  Combined choirs and military band, conducted by Alan Bush
Publication: WMA Vocal score © 1948
Manuscript: British Library, MS. Mus. 411, ff. 85-87

DOWLAND, J.

Three Pavanes
From '[Three] Lacrymae or Seven Teares', figured in Seven
  Passionate Pavanes

Arranged for string orchestra (10 solo string instruments)
First performance: London, Wigmore Hall, 15 June 1941
  Members of the London String Orchestra, conducted by
  Alan Bush
Manuscript: British Library, MS. Mus. 427, ff. 64-74
Bibliography: *The Times*, 17 June 1941, 6 (Anon.)

Droylesden Wakes

Arranged for mixed chorus (SATB) and piano
Publication: J. Williams Ltd. © 1953 (*Ten English Folksongs*)

DUNSTABLE, J.

O Rosa Bella
Arranged for men's voices (TBarB)

Easter Bells

Norwegian song
Arranged for female (SSA) or mixed voices (SATB)

Ege Denizi: March (Turkish)

Arranged for mixed chorus (SATB) with flute, clarinet, tenor
  trombone, percussion and piano
Manuscript: British Library, MS. Mus. 428, ff. 117-118

EISLER, H.

Death and Destruction
Arranged for unison chorus with flute, clarinet, trumpet, tenor
  trombone, percussion and piano

England Arise

Arranged for mixed chorus (SATB) and band
First performance: London, Wembley Stadium, 2 July 1938
  Combined choirs and band, conducted by Alan Bush
Manuscript: British Library, MS. Mus. 398, ff. 61-87

FIELD, J.

Nocturne No.14
Arranged for string orchestra
First performance: London, Aeolian Hall, 28 October 1939
  London String Orchestra, conducted by Alan Bush

First broadcast performance: London, BBC Home Service, 4 August 1945
  London String Orchestra, conducted by Alan Bush
Publication: Francis, Day & Hunter. Full score © 1954
Bibliography: *Musical Times*, 80 (November 1939), 775-6 (WG)

Rondo (Piano Sonata in C minor, Opus1)
Arranged for string orchestra
First performance: London, Aeolian Hall, 28 October 1939
  London String Orchestra, conducted by Alan Bush
First broadcast performance: London, BBC Home Service, 20 December
  1942. London String Orchestra, conducted by Alan Bush
Manuscript: British Library, MS. Mus. 427, ff. 75-83

Freedom on the Wallaby
Traditional Australian song arranged for mixed chorus (SATB) and piano
Text: Henry Lawson
Publication: WMA © 1965 (*From the Five Continents*)

GABRIELI, A.

Ricercar a 8 per Sonar
Arranged for string orchestra
First performance: London, Wigmore Hall, 30 January 1939
  London String Orchestra, conducted by Alan Bush
Publication: Skidmore Music Co., New York. Score © [1960]

Geordie
Arranged for mixed chorus (SATB) and piano
First performance: London, French Institute, 13 December 1955
  WMA Singers, conducted by Bernard Stevens
Publication: J. Williams Ltd. © 1953 (*Ten English Folksongs*)

God Save the People
Arranged for mixed chorus (SATB) and band
First performance: London, Wembley Stadium, 2 July 1938
  Combined choirs and band, conducted by Alan Bush
Manuscript: British Library, MS. Mus. 398, ff. 61-87

Greensleeves
Traditional English song arranged for piano solo
First performance: London, Broadcasting House, 15 March 1961
  Alan Bush (piano) in the BBC Programme 'Roundabout'

Manuscript: British Library, MS. Mus. 428, ff.125

HANDEL, G.F.

Concerto Grosso in A minor
Continuo part realised by AB
First performance: London, Wigmore Hall, 15 June 1941
  London String Orchestra, conducted by Alan Bush
Bibliography: *The Times*, 17 June 1941, 6 (Anon.)

Concerto Grosso No. 7 in Bb
Continuo part realised by AB
First performance: London, Aeolian Hall, 2 November 1941
  London String Orchestra, conducted by Alan Bush
Manuscript: British Library, MS. Mus. 428, ff. 14-20
Bibliography: *The Times*, 4 November 1941,6 (Anon.)

Concerto Grosso No. 8 in C minor
Continuo part realised by AB
First performance: London, Aeolian Hall, 2 November 1941
  London String Orchestra, conducted by Alan Bush
Manuscript: British Library, MS. Mus. 428, ff. 21-25
Bibliography: *The Times*, 4 November 1941, 6 (Anon.)

Hanging Johnny
Arranged for mixed chorus (SAB) and piano
Publication: J. Williams Ltd. © 1955 (*20 Sing for Pleasure Songs*)

Hares on the Mountain
Arranged for mixed chorus (SAB) and piano
First performance: London, French Institute, 13 December 1955
  WMA Singers, conducted by Bernard Stevens
Publication: J. Williams Ltd. © 1955 (*20 Sing for Pleasure Songs*)

HASSLER, H.L.

Ricercar VII Toni
Arranged for string orchestra
First performance: London, Wigmore Hall, 18 February 1940
  London String Orchestra, conducted by Alan Bush
Bibliography: *Musical Times*, 81 (March 1940), 132 (W. McNaught);
  The Times, 20 February 1940, 6 (Anon)

HAYDN, J.

Waltzes: numbers 1 and 4 (*12 German Waltzes*)
Arranged for string orchestra
First performance: London, Wigmore Hall, 30 January 1939
  London String Orchestra, conducted by Alan Bush
Bibliography: *Musical Times*, 80 (March 1939), 222-3 (MMS)

HAYS, L. and SEEGER, P.

If I Had a Hammer
Arranged for unison voices and piano
Publication: WMA © 1950

Henry Martin

Arranged for mixed chorus (SATB) and piano
First performance: London, Conway Hall, 22 March 1948
  WMA Singers, conducted by Alan Bush
Publication: J. Williams Ltd. © 1953 (*10 English Folksongs*)

HENSELT, A.

Valse Gracieuse
Arranged for violin and piano
Manuscript: British Library, MS. Mus. 428, ff. 26-32

HERMLIN, S.

Song of the Workers (Lied der Werktätigen)
Arranged for flute, clarinet, trumpet, tenor trombone, percussion
  and piano

Text: Stephen Hermlin
Manuscript: British Library, MS. Mus. 428, ff. 33-34

High Barbary

Arranged for baritone solo, mixed chorus (SAB) and piano
Publication: J. Williams Ltd. © 1955 (*20 Sing for Pleasure Songs*)

(The) Hiring Song

Arranged for mixed chorus (SAB) and piano
Publication: J. Williams Ltd. © 1955 (*20 Sing for Pleasure Songs*)

HUGHES, John

Cwm Rhonda
Hymn tune arranged for mixed chorus (SATB) and military band
First performance: London, Wembley Stadium, 2 July 1938
  Combined choirs and band, conducted by Alan Bush
Manuscript: British Library, MS. Mus. 398, ff. 61-87

HUMMEL, J.N.

Waltz (No.3 of Waltzes for the Pianoforte)
Arranged for string orchestra
First performance: London, Wigmore Hall, 30 January 1939
  London String Orchestra, conducted by Alan Bush
Bibliography: *Musical Times*, 80 (March 1939), 222-3 (MMS)

I Will Give My Love an Apple

Arranged for mixed chorus (SAB) and piano
Publication: J. Williams Ltd. © 1955 (*20 Sing for Pleasure Songs*)

Ilkley Moor

Arranged for mixed chorus (SAB) and piano
Publication: J. Williams Ltd. © 1955 (*20 Sing for Pleasure Songs*)

IRELAND, J.

These things shall be (1936-37)
For baritone solo, mixed chorus (SATB) and orchestra
Text: John Addington Symonds
Commissioned by: The BBC to celebrate the coronation of King
  George VI and Queen Elizabeth in May 1937
Orchestrated by Alan Bush
First (public) performance: London, Queen's Hall, 1 December 1937
  Dennis Noble (baritone), the BBC Choral Society and the BBC
  Symphony Orchestra, conducted by Adrian Boult
Manuscript: British Library, Add. MS. 52892A (full score); 52892B
  (sketches and short score)
Bibliography: *Musical Times*, 79 (January 1938), 57 (W. McNaught)

(The) Isley Reapers' Song

Arranged for mixed chorus (SATB)
First performance: Southend, SE Essex Technical College, 20 September
  1952. WMA Singers, conducted by Alan Bush

It's a Long Way to Tipperary
Arranged for mixed chorus (SATB) and military band
First performance: London, Royal Albert Hall, 1 April 1939
  Massed choirs and band, conducted by Alan Bush
Manuscript: British Library, MS. Mus. 404-405

JENKINS, J.

Fantasia
Arranged for string orchestra
First performance: London, Aeolian Hall, 28 October 1939
  London String Orchestra, conducted by Alan Bush
Bibliography: *Musical Times*, 80 (November 1939), 775-6 (WG)

Johnnie Sangster
Arranged for soprano solo, mixed chorus (SATB) and piano
First performance: London, Conway Hall, 22 March 1948
  WMA Singers, conducted by Alan Bush
Publication: J. Williams Ltd. © 1953 (*10 English Folk Songs*)

Keep the Home Fires Burning
Arranged for mixed chorus and military band
First performance: London, Royal Albert Hall, 1 April 1939
  Massed choirs and band, conducted by Alan Bush
Manuscript: British Library, MS. Mus. 404-405

KHACHATURIAN, A.

Song of the Soviet Women
Arranged for flute and piano
Manuscript: British Library, MS. Mus. 428, ff. 35-41

Koki Kinoshita ('Against the Atom Bomb')
[Song of Hiroshima] arranged for mixed chorus (SATB) and piano
English words by Ewan MacColl
Publication: WMA © 1965 (*From the Five Continents*)

KREIN, A.A.

Dance for piano (Opus 44, No.3)
Arranged for string orchestra
First performance: Ilford, Savoy Cinema, 25 July 1943
  London String Orchestra, conducted by Alan Bush

Manuscript: British Library, MS. Mus. 427, ff. 84-94

Land of Freedom

Russian song arranged for mixed chorus (SATB) and orchestra
Note: This song is mentioned in a letter to Steuart Wilson at the BBC,
dated 12 February 1945. The score and parts were said to be in the
possession of the Nottingham Harmonic Society, for whom they
were prepared

LANNER, J.

Waltzes (numbers 2 and 3 of the Pesther Waltzes, Opus 93)
Arranged for string orchestra
First performance: London, Wigmore Hall, 30 January 1939
  London String Orchestra, conducted by Alan Bush
Bibliography: *Musical Times*, 80 (March 1939), 222-3 (MMS)

(The) Lark in the Morning

English folk song arranged for mixed chorus (SAB) and piano
Publication: J. Williams Ltd. © 1955 (*20 Sing for Pleasure Songs*)

LAWES, W.

Fantasia No.7
Arranged for string orchestra
First performance: London, Aeolian Hall, 28 October 1939
  London String Orchestra, conducted by Alan Bush
Bibliography: *Musical Times*, 80 (November 1939), 775-6 (WG)

LIAPUNOV, Sergei

Nuit d'été and Berceuse (two of the *Transcendental Studies*)
Re-written and arranged for piano (Opus 90)

(The) Lincolnshire Poacher

English folksong arranged for mixed chorus (SAB) and piano
First performance: London, Conway Hall, 22 March 1948
  WMA Singers, conducted by Alan Bush
Publication: J. Williams Ltd. © 1955 (*20 Sing for Pleasure Songs*)

(The) Little Turtle Dove

Arranged for male chorus (TBarB) and piano
Publication: J. Williams Ltd. © 1955 (*20 Sing for Pleasure Songs*)

LOCKE, M. and GIBBONS, C.

Dances from *Cupid and Death*
Arranged for string orchestra

Los Campesinos

Arranged for mixed chorus (SATB) with flute, clarinet, trumpet, tenor
 trombone, percussion and piano

Lowlands, My Lowlands

Arranged for mixed chorus (SAB) and piano
First performance: London, Conway Hall, 22 March 1948
 WMA Singers, conducted by Alan Bush
Publication: J. Williams Ltd. © 1955 (*20 Sing for Pleasure Songs*)

Lucky Locket

Arranged for mixed chorus (SATB) and military band
First performance: London, Wembley Stadium, 2 July 1938
 Combined choirs and band, conducted by Alan Bush
Manuscript: British Library, MS. Mus. 398, ff. 9-13

LULLY, J-B.

Chaconne (from his opera *Rowland*)
Arranged for string orchestra
First performance: London, BBC Home Service, 20 July 1947
 London String Orchestra, conducted by Alan Bush
Publication: Francis, Day & Hunter. Full score © 1954

MAKAROV-RATAKIN, K.D.

Romance (Opus 1, No.4 for piano)
Arranged for string orchestra
First performance: Ilford, Savoy Cinema, 25 July 1943
 London String Orchestra, conducted by Alan Bush
Manuscript: British Library, MS. Mus. 427, ff. 95-97

Melodies of 15 English Folk Songs (13 with words)

Transcribed from various sources
Manuscript: British Library, MS. Mus. 428, ff. 126-127
 (Melodies are grouped by mode)

Melodies of Scotland
Transcribed from Thomson's The Select Melodies of Scotland
  (5v, Edinburgh, Thomson, 1822)
Manuscript: British Library, MS. Mus. 428, ff. 119-124 (October 1981)

Men of Harlech
Arranged for mixed chorus (SATB) and military band
First performance: London, Wembley Stadium, 2 July 1938
  Combined choirs and band, conducted by Alan Bush
Manuscript: British Library, MS. Mus. 399, ff. 40-43

MENDELSSOHN, F

The Bees Wedding (*Songs without Words*, Opus 67, No.4)
Arranged for string orchestra
First performance: Watford, Town Hall, 1 July 1947
  London String Orchestra, conducted by Alan Bush
First broadcast performance: London, BBC Light Programme, 1 August
  1947. London String Orchestra, conducted by Alan Bush
Manuscript: British Library, MS. Mus. 427, ff. 98-101

Romance in Ab for String Quartet, Opus 44, No.4)
Arranged for string orchestra
First performance: London, BBC Home Service, 6 July 1947
  London String Orchestra, conducted by Alan Bush
Publication: John Fields Music Co. Full score © 1960

Waltzes
Arranged for string orchestra
First performance: London, Wigmore Hall, 30 January 1939
  London String Orchestra, conducted by Alan Bush
Bibliography: *Musical Times*, 80 (March 1939), 222-3 (MMS)

MEYER, E.G.

Two movements from his opera *Reiter der Nacht* [Meditation from
  Scene 1 and Duet from Scene 7]
Arranged for mixed voices (SATB) and piano
Text in English and German
Manuscript: British Library, MS. Mus. 428, ff. 42-63

MONTEHUS, G.

The Young Guard
Text by Garton Montehus; English version by Nancy Bush
Arranged for mixed choir (SATB) and piano

MOSZKOWSKI, M.

Berceuse (Opus 38, No.4) from *Four Pieces for Piano*
Arranged for string orchestra
Manuscript: British Library, MS. Mus. 428, ff. 71-72

En Automne (Opus 26, No.4) from *Eight Characteristic Pieces for Piano*
Arranged for string orchestra
Manuscript: British Library, MS. Mus. 428, ff. 64-70

MOZART, W.A.

Adagio and Fugue
Arranged for string orchestra
First performance: London. Wigmore Hall, 17 December 1940
  London String Orchestra, conducted by Alan Bush

(The) Mulberry Bush

Arranged for mixed chorus (SATB) and military band
First performance: London, Wembley Stadium, 2 July 1938
  Combined choirs and band, conducted by Alan Bush
Manuscript: British Library, MS. Mus. 398, ff..59-60

MURADELI, V.

Lenin in Siberia
Arranged for mixed choir (SATB) and orchestra
English version (from the Russian) by Nancy Bush

ONSLOW, G.

Two movements from his *String Quartet No. 12* (Opus 34)
Arranged for string orchestra

PACHELBEL, J.

Chorale-Prelude "Ach Herr, mich armen Sünder"
Arranged for string orchestra
First performance: London, Aeolian Hall, 6 December 1941

London String Orchestra, conducted by Alan Bush
Manuscript: British Library, MS. Mus. 427, 45v-47

People of England
Arranged for mixed chorus (SATB) and military band
First performance: London, Royal Albert Hall, 1 April 1939
  Massed choirs and band, conducted by Alan Bush
Manuscript: British Library, MS. Mus. 404-405

The People Sing
Revolutionary songs arranged for piano duet

PICON, ?

Diabolero
Arranged for military band
First performance: BBC, Home Service, 3 June 1941
  The BBC Military Band, conducted by P.S.G. O'Donnell

PIERNE, G.

Nocturne No.1 for piano
Arranged for string orchestra
Manuscript: British Library, MS. Mus. 428, ff. 73-77

PURCELL, H.

Fairest Isle (*King Arthur*)
Arranged for mixed chorus (SATB) and piano
Text: John Dryden
First performance: Wood Green, Town Hall, 4 April 1964
  Choirs from Alexandra Choral Society and local choirs
  with Geoff Vince (piano), conducted by Alan Bush

Fantasia
In three, four and five voices
Arranged for string orchestra
First performance: London, Wigmore Hall, 30 January 1939
  London String Orchestra, conducted by Alan Bush
Bibliography: *Musical Times*, 80 (March 1939), 222-3 (MMS)

Fantasia
In three voices

Arranged for string orchestra
First broadcast performance: London, BBC Home Service, 14
  September 1947. London String Orchestra, conducted by
  Alan Bush

Fantasia
Upon one note
Arranged for string orchestra
First performance: London, Wigmore Hall, 15 June 1941
  London String Orchestra, conducted by Alan Bush
First broadcast performance: London, BBC Home Service, 9 May 1946
  London String Orchestra, conducted by Alan Bush
Bibliography: *The Times*, 17 June 1941, 6 (Anon.)

Hark, the Echoing Air! (*The Fairy Queen*)
Arranged for soprano, and strings, the basso continuo realised by AB
Manuscript: British Library, MS. Mus. 428, ff. 78-86

Hornpipe (*The Old Bachelor*)
Arranged (1) for string orchestra and (2) with Air and Minuet arranged for
  Mandoline I and II, Mandola and Gitarre
Publisher (No.2): Veb Friedrich Hofmeister, Leipzig (n.d.) as *Drei Kleine
  Spielstucke*

Hornpipe on a Ground (*The Married Beau*)
Arranged for string orchestra

In Nomine
Arranged for string orchestra
First performance: London, Wigmore Hall, 30 January 1939
  London String Orchestra, conducted by Alan Bush
Bibliography: *Musical Times*, 80 (March 1939), 222-3 (MMS)

Overture (*The Rival Sisters*)
Arranged for string orchestra
Publication: Francis, Day & Hunter. Full score © 1954

Overture (*The Virtuous Wife*)
Arranged for string orchestra
Publication: Francis, Day & Hunter. Full score © 1954

Sonatas 2 (in Eb, Adagio) and 6 (in G minor, Adagio) for 2 violins and bass
Arranged for string orchestra
First performance: London, Wigmore Hall, 30 January 1939
  London String Orchestra, conducted by Alan Bush
Bibliography: *Musical Times*, 80 (March 1939), 222-3 (MMS)

Suite: The Fairy Queen
Edited and arranged for small orchestra

Symphony (Act II)
Rondo
Hornpipe
Dance of the Haymakers
Dance of the Followers of Night
Monkey's Dance
Chaconne

2 oboes, 2 trumpets, harp, strings and continuo
First performance : Bucharest, 2 December 1955
  Romanian State Philharmonic Orchestra, conducted by Alan Bush
Publication: J. Williams Ltd. Full score © 1959

When I am Laid in Earth (*Dido and Aeneas*)
Arranged for string orchestra

RAFF, J.

Evening ("Abends" – No. 12 of Frühlingsboten for piano, Opus 55)
Arranged for violin and piano
Manuscript: British Library, MS. Mus. 428, ff. 87-93

Romance and Villanella
Arranged for violin, cello and piano
Manuscript: British Library, MS. Mus. 428, ff. 94-107

Rebel Song
Arranged for mixed chorus (SATB) and military band
First performance: London, Wembley Stadium, 2 July 1938
  Combined choirs and band, conducted by Alan Bush
Manuscript: British Library, MS, Mus. 398, ff. 61-87

(The) Red Flag
Text: J. Connell
(1) Arranged for mixed chorus (SATB) and piano
Publication: The Left Song Book (Gollancz © 1938)
(2) Arranged for mixed chorus (SATB) and military band
First performance: London, Wembley Stadium, 2 July 1938
  Combined choirs and band, conducted by Alan Bush
Manuscript: British Library, MS. Mus. 399, ff. 34-37
(3) Arranged for unaccompanied mixed chorus (SATB)
First performance: London, Royal Albert Hall, 30 March 1948
  Combined choirs conducted by Alan Bush
Manuscript: British Library, MS. Mus. 411, ff. 74-91

RETAKIN, ?

Romance
Arranged for string orchestra
First performance: Ilford, Savoy Cinema, 25 July 1943
  London String Orchestra, conducted by Alan Bush

RIES, F.

Waltz in E flat
Arranged for string orchestra
First performance: London, Wigmore Hall, 30 January 1939
  London String Orchestra, conducted by Alan Bush
Bibliography: *Musical Times*, 80 (March 1939), 222-3 (MMS)

Rise up now, ye Shepherds
French carol arranged for mixed voices (SATB)
Publication: Novello & Co. Ltd. © 1963 (*Sing Nowell*)

ROBERTS, Alfred

The Land it is the Landlord's
Song arranged for (1) Festival of Music for the People,
  Royal Albert Hall, 1 April 1939
  Massed choirs and band, conducted by Alan Bush
Manuscript: British Library, MS. Mus. 404-405
(2) Fifty Years Fighting: Film about *Labour Monthly* (1970)
Manuscript: British Library, MS. Mus. 414, ff. 7-9

Rosetta and her Gay Plough Boy
Arranged for mixed voices (SATB)
Publication: J. Williams Ltd. © 1953 (*10 English Folk Songs*)

ROTAS, Y.

E.A.M. Song
Arranged for two-part or unison chorus
Publication: WMA Vocal score © 1949 (*Songs from Greece*)

ROUGET De Lisle, C.J.

La Marseillaise
Arranged for mixed chorus and military band
First performance: London, Wembley Stadium, 2 July 1938
  Combined choirs and band, conducted by Alan Bush
Manuscript: British Library, MS. Mus. 399, ff. 46-49

Russian Funeral March from the Revolution of 1905
Arranged (1) for brass and percussion, (2) organ
Manuscript: British Library, MS. Mus. 427, ff. 149-153, and
(3) Military band
First performance: London, Royal Albert Hall, 1 April 1939
  Festival Wind Band, conducted by Alan Bush
Manuscript: British Library, MS. Mus. 404-405 (band parts)

SCHÖFFERS, P.

Liederbuch (1513): 1-Mich trubt schwelich (Anon) and 2-Ach Un fall
  Gross (Wolff)
Arranged for string orchestra
First performance: London, Wigmore Hall, 18 February 1940
  London String Orchestra, conducted by Alan Bush
Manuscript: No.2, British Library, MS. Mus. 427, ff. 107-8
Bibliography: *Musical Times*, 81 (March 1940), 132 (W. McNaught);
  The Times, 20 February 1940, 6 (Anon.)

SCHUMANN, R.

Five movements from *Carnival* (Opus 9)
Arranged for full orchestra (c.1925?)

Preamble
Harlequin
Eusebius
Chopin
Reconnaissance

2+1.2.2.2/4.2 cornets 3 trbns.0/timpani percussion (2) and strings
Manuscript: British Library, MS. Mus. 427, ff. 1-35

SCHÜTT, E.

Valse Lente for piano (Opus 17, No.2)
Edited by A.D. Bush
Manuscript: British Library, MS. Mus. 428, ff. 108-111

Scots, Wha Hae
Scottish folk song arranged for mixed chorus
Text: R. Burns
First performance: London, Wembley Stadium, 2 July 1938
  Combined choirs and band, conducted by Alan Bush
Publication: The Left Song Book (Gollancz © 1938)
Manuscript: British Library, MS. Mus. 399, ff. 38-39

(The) Scrawny Black Farmer
Arranged for mixed chorus (SATB) and piano
First performance: London, Conway Hall, 22 March 1948
  WMA Singers, conducted by Alan Bush
Publication: J. Williams Ltd. © 1953 (*10 English Folk Songs*)

(A) Seaman's Life
Arranged for mixed chorus (SAB) and piano
First performance: Southend, SE Essex Technical College,
  20 September 1952. WMA Singers, conducted by Alan Bush
Publication: J. Williams Ltd. © 1955 (*20 Sing for Pleasure Songs*)

SENFL, L.

Carmina No.8: Lamentation and No.10: Carmen in re
Arranged for string orchestra
First performance: London, Wigmore Hall, 18 February 1940
  London String Orchestra, conducted by Alan Bush
Manuscript: British Library, MS. Mus. 427, ff. 102-106

Bibliography: *Musical Times*, 81 (March 1940), 132 (W. McNaught);
  The Times, 20 February 1940, 6 (Anon.)

She Walked Thro' the Fair

Folk song arranged for mixed chorus (SATB) and piano
First performance: London, Conway Hall, 22 March 1948
  WMA Singers, conducted by Alan Bush

Sheep-Shearing

Arranged for mixed chorus (SATB) and piano
Publication: J. Williams Ltd. © 1953 (*10 English Folk Songs*)

(The) Shoemaker

Arranged for baritone solo, mixed chorus (SATB) and piano
First performance: London, Conway Hall, 22 March 1948
  WMA Singers, conducted by Alan Bush
Publication: J. Williams Ltd. © 1953 (*10 English Folk Songs*)

SHOSTAKOVICH, D.

Preludes 21 and 22 (*24 Preludes for piano*)
Arranged for flute and piano
Manuscript: British Library, MS. Mus. 428, ff. 112-116

Song of the Peatbog Soldiers

Arranged for unaccompanied male voices (TTBB)
Written in a German concentration camp
First performance: London, Royal Albert Hall, 1 April 1939
  Festival chorus conducted by Alan Bush
Publication: WMA. Vocal score [n.d.]
Manuscript: British Library, MS, Mus. 404-405

(The) Sons of Liberty

Folk song arranged for mixed chorus (SATB) and piano
First performance: London, Conway House, 22 March 1948
  WMA Singers, conducted by Alan Bush

Soviet Cradle Song

Arranged for female voices (SA) and piano
Note: In a letter from the Performing Right Society, dated 7 July 1943,
  a publication ('Sing and Learn') is mentioned which was to
  include the *Soviet Cradle Song*, together with *Song of the*

Coming Day, Till Right is Done and an arrangement of *I went to 'tlanta*. This, however, has not been traced

(The) Spermwhale Fishery

Arranged for mezzo soprano solo, mixed chorus (SATB) and piano
First performance: Southend, SE Essex Technical College, 20
  September 1952. WMA Singers, conducted by Alan Bush
Publication: J. Williams Ltd. © 1955 (*20 Sing for Pleasure Songs*)

Step it Out

Red Army song arranged for mixed chorus (SATB)
Note: This may have been arranged for the WMA Singers

Steppeland

Russian song arranged for mixed chorus (SATB) and orchestra

STERNDALE-BENNETT, W.

Allegro Agitato (*6 Studies for piano*, Opus 11, No.6)
Arranged for string orchestra
First performance: London, Aeolian Hall, 28 October 1939
  London String Orchestra, conducted by Alan Bush
First broadcast performance: London, BBC Home Service, 4 August 1945
  London String Orchestra, conducted by Alan Bush
Manuscript: British Library, MS. Mus. 427, ff. 58-63
Bibliography: *Musical Times*, 80 (November 1939), 775-6 (WG)

Nocturne No. 14 in C
Arranged for string orchestra

Rondo (*Sonata in C minor for piano*, Opus 1)
Arranged for string orchestra

Serenade (*Chamber Trio*, Opus 26)
Arrange for string orchestra
First performance: London, Aeolian Hall, 28 October 1939
  London String Orchestra, conducted by Alan Bush
Publication: Francis, Day and Hunter. Full score © 1954
Bibliography: *Musical Times*, 80 (November 1939), 775-6 (WG)

STRAUSS, J. I and II

Waltzes
Arranged for string orchestra
First performance: London, Wigmore Hall, 30 January 1939
  London String Orchestra, conducted by Alan Bush
Bibliography: *Musical Times,* 80 (March 1939), 222-3 (MMS)

SUK, J.

Meditation on an old Bohemian Choral
Arranged for string orchestra
First performance: London, Wigmore Hall, 25 March 1939
  London String Orchestra, conducted by Alan Bush
Bibliography: *The Times*, 27 March 1939, 19 (Anon.)

Sumer is Icumen In: The Reading Rota

Arranged for unaccompanied mixed chorus (SSATBB)
Text translated by: John Hoyland
New version of text by Nancy Bush
First performance: London, King George's Hall (WC2), 16 June 1949
  WMA Singers, conducted by Alan Bush
Publication: WMA © 1963 (*English Song Series, No. 5*)

(The) Sweet Nightingale

Arranged for mixed chorus (SSATB) and piano
Publication: J. Williams Ltd. © 1953 (*10 English Folk Songs*)

Tachanka

Red Army song arranged for mixed chorus (SATB)
Note: This may have been made for the WMA Singers

(The) Tarrier's Song

Arranged for baritone or bass solo, mixed chorus (SAB) and piano
Publication: J. Williams Ltd. © 1955 (*20 Sing for Pleasure Songs*)

TCHAIKOVSKY, P.

Serenade in C
Arranged for string orchestra
First performance: Cambridge, Arts Theatre, 29 October 1939
  London String Orchestra, conducted by Alan Bush

Three Negro Songs
Arranged for solo tenor and unaccompanied male chorus (TTBB)
Text: Traditional American
Manuscript: British Library, MS. Mus. 424, ff. 38-50: Draft scores
  in pencil; score in ink
  ff. 41-44 'Hurry on, my weary soul' (Negro slave song)
  ff. 45-46 'Many thousand go' (Negro slave song)
  ff. 47-50 'It makes a long time man feel bad' (Negro prison song)

Time for Us to Leave Her
Folk song arranged for mixed chorus (SATB)
First performance: Southend, SE Essex Technical College, 20 September
  1952. WMA Singers, conducted by Alan Bush

Tom, Tom, the Piper's Son
Arranged for mixed chorus (SATB) and military band
First performance: London, Wembley Stadium, 2 July 1938
  Combined choirs and band, conducted by Alan Bush
Manuscript: British Library, MS. Mus. 398, ff. 9-13

Two Fantasies from a Liederbuch of 1513
Arranged for string orchestra
First performance: London, Wigmore Hall, 18 February 1940
  London String Orchestra, conducted by Alan Bush
Bibliography: *Musical Times*, 81 (March 1940), 132 (W. McNaught);
  The Times, 20 February 1940, 6 (Anon.)

Two Spanish Songs
Arranged for cello and piano
First performance: B. Rickelmann (cello) and AB (piano)

United States Negroes' Civil Right Campaign Song: We Shall Overcome
Arranged for mixed chorus and piano
Publication: WMA © 1965 (*From the Five Continents*)

Varsavyanka
Arranged for mixed chorus (SATB) with flute, clarinet, trumpet, tenor
  trombone, percussion and piano

VARSCHOVIANKA, ?

Whirlwinds of Danger
Arranged for mixed voices and piano
Text adapted by Randall Swingler
Publication: The Left Song Book (Gollancz © 1938)

(The) Water is Wide

Arranged for mixed chorus (SAB) and piano
Publication: J. Williams Ltd. © 1955 (*20 Sing for Pleasure Songs*)

Way Down Upon the Swanee River

Arranged for mixed chorus (SATB) and military band
First performance: London, Wembley Stadium, 2 July 1938
  Combined choirs and band, conducted by Alan Bush
Manuscript: British Library, MS. Mus. 399, ff. 56-57

(The) Wearing of the Green

Arranged for mixed chorus (SATB) and military band
First performance: London, Wembley Stadium, 2 July 1938
  Combined choirs and band, conducted by Alan Bush
Manuscript: British Library, MS. Mus. 398, ff. 44-45

We're Low

Arranged for mixed voices (SATB) and military band
First performance: London, Royal Albert Hall, 1 April 1939
  Massed choirs and band, conducted by Alan Bush
Manuscript: British Library, MS. Mus. 404-405

Westron Wynd

Arranged for mixed voices (SATB) and piano
First performance: London, Conway Hall, 22 March 1948
  WMA Singers, conducted by Alan Bush

WOLF, H.

Italian Serenade
Arranged for string orchestra
First performance: London, Wigmore Hall, 25 March 1939
  London String Orchestra, conducted by Alan Bush
Bibliography: *The Times*, 27 March 1939, 19 (Anon.)

Workers' March (John Brown's Body)
Arranged for mixed voices (SATB) and military band
First performance: London, Wembley Stadium, 2 July 1938
  Combined choirs and band, conducted by Alan Bush
Manuscript: British Library, MS. Mus. 398, ff. 61-87

Yankee Doodle
Arranged for mixed voices (SATB) and military band
First performance: London, Wembley Stadium, 2 July 1938
  Combined choirs and band, conducted by Alan Bush
Manuscript: British Library, MS. Mus. 399, ff. 54-55

Young Comrades' Song
Arranged for mixed voices (SATB) and military band
First performance: London, Wembley Stadium, 2 July 1938
  Combined choirs and band, conducted by Alan Bush
Manuscript: British Library, MS. Mus. 399, ff. 62-66

Young Gilderoy
Arranged for mixed voices (SATB) and piano
First performance: London, Conway Hall, 22 March 1948
  WMA Singers, conducted by Alan Bush
Publication: J. Williams Ltd. © 1953 (*10 English Folk Songs*)

(The) Youth Railway
Slav youth song arranged for 2-part or unison chorus
English text by John Manifold
Publication: WMA Vocal score © 1947 (*Songs from the New Europe*)

General bibliography

Alwyn, W. "Notes in Retropect", in Stevenson, R. (ed.), *Time Remembered – Alan Bush: an 80th birthday symposium*. Kidderminster, Bravura Publications, 1981, 111-13

Amis, J. "Alan Bush: An Appreciation", Alan Bush Music Trust Website

——— "Bishop's Parlour and Speaker's Corner", in Stevenson, R. (ed.), *Time Remembered – Alan Bush: an 80th birthday symposium*. Kidderminster, Bravura Publications, 1981, 119-21

——— "Bush at 70", *Music and Musicians*, 19 (December 1970), 28-9

——— "Man of the People", *The Listener*, 114 No.2940 (19 and 26 December 1985), 65

——— "Young Composers", *Vogue*, October 1950, 126+128+130

Anderson, M. "Alan Bush", Alan Bush Music Trust Website

Anderson, W.R. "Alan Bush, born 1900", *Music Teacher*, 29 (August 1950), 361+

——— Review of Alan Bush's 'Music in the Soviet Union', *Musical Times*, 85 (February 1944), 48

Anon. "Alan Bush" [Handel Prize], *Musical Events*, 17 (November 1962), 30

Anon. "Alan Bush im Pädagogischen Institut Zwickau", *Musik in Der Schule*, 18 No. 5 (1967), 19-20

Anon. "Alan Bush na 70 godini", *Bulgarska Muzika*, 22 No.1 (1971), 91

Anon. [Alan Bush plays Bach at the RAM Spring Concert], *Musical Times*, 63 (April 1922), 270

Anon. "Alan Bush 75", *Musik und Gesellschaft*, 25 (December 1975), 765-6

Anon. "Alan Bush: A Portrait" (Composer of the Month), *London Philharmonic Post*, 4 (July-August 1949), 3-4

Anon. "Alan Bush at 75", *Music and Musicians*, 24 (December 1975), 18+

Anon. "Alan Bush is 60", *Musical Events*, 16 (November 1961), 26

Anon. "Alan Bush's 50th Birthday", *Musical Times*, 92 (February 1951), 84

Anon. BBC bans [Alan Bush's compositions banned from broadcasting], *The Times*, 8 March 1941, 3

Anon. "Composers of Today" [Portrait], *Music Parade*, 2 No.3 (1950), opposite page 1

Anon. "Druz'ya iz Anglii", *Sovetskaya Muzyka*, 27 (December 1963), 86-7

Anon. "Ein englischner Freund des deutschen Volkes", *Musik und Gesellschaft*, 11 (January 1961), 51-2

Anon. "Guests of Soviet Composers", *World News*, 5, No.6 (1963), 135

Anon. "In Honour of Alan Bush", *The Times*, 20 November 1961, 14

Anon. "Iz otklikov na anketu", *Sovetskaya Muzyka*, 36 (January 1972), 57

Anon. "Living British Composers", *Hinrichsen Yearbook*, 6 (1949-1950), 121-2

Anon. "London Philharmonic Orchestra: Concerts", *The Times*, 8 January 1945, 8

Anon. "Mr Alan Bush", *The Times*, 5 December 1927, 12

Anon. "Notes of the Day", *Monthly Musical Record*, 81 (February 1951), 31

Anon. "Obituary: Alan Bush", *The Daily Telegraph*, 3 November 1995, 31

Anon. "Obituary: Alan Bush", *Gramophone*, 73 (January 1996), 12

Anon. "Obituary: Alan Bush", *Notes*, 52 No.4 (1996), 1121

Anon. "Obituary: Alan Bush", *Opera*, 47 (February 1996), 165-6

Anon. "Obituary: Alan Bush", *Opera News*, 60 (13 April 1996)

Anon. "Obituary: Alan Bush", *Opera Quarterly*, 13 No. 3 (1997), 5

Anon. "Obituary: Alan Bush", *Sing Out*, 4 No.1 (1996), 32

Anon. "Obituary: Alan Bush", *The Times*, 4 November 1995, 23

Anon. "Portrait: Alan Bush", *British Music*, 22 (2000), between 38-9

Anon. "Queen's Hall", *The Times*, 6 November 1940, 6

Anon. "Songs by Alan Bush", *The Times*, 8 January 1945, 8

Anon. "Students' Concert", *The Times*, 6 January 1953, 9

Anon. "U nas v gostyakh uchastniki Vsemirnogo kongressa za vseobschchee razoruzhenie i mir", *Sovetskaya Muzyka*, 26 (September 1962), 131-2

Armstrong, T. "Alan Bush as a Teacher", in Stevenson, R. (ed.) *Time Remembered-Alan Bush: an 80th birthday symposium*. Kidderminster, Bravura Publications, 1981, 124-5

Barry, M. "Alan Bush", *Music and Musicians*, 26 (February 1978), 52-3

——— "Socialist music" (WMA Concert), *Music and Musicians*, 24 (May 1976), 52+

Bednall, D. "The Complete Organ Works of Alan Bush", *Clarion*, 8 (2005-2006), 4-5

Berry, J. "Memories of Alan Bush and Ernst Mayer", *Clarion*, 8 (2005-2006), 6

Blank, G. "Zwichau: Vortag Alan Bushs im Padagogischen Institut", *Musik und Gesellschaft*, 17 (April 1967), 279

Boughton, R. "Close Contact with the People", in WMA, Tribute to Alan Bush on his 50th birthday: a symposium. London, WMA, 1950, 20

Bowers, T. "Alan Bush as a Composition Teacher", Alan Bush Music Trust Website

Bowers, T. "Discovering Alan Bush's Late Works", *Clarion*, 5 (2002-2003), [1-2]

————— "The Piano Sonatas of Alan Bush", *Clarion*, 8 (2005-2006), [1-2]

Bowman, A. "A Matter of Talent", in Stevenson, R. (ed.) *Time Remembered – Alan Bush: an 80th birthday symposium*. Kidderminster, Bravura Publications, 1981, 126-31

Bush, A. "Adventure in Music", *Housewife*, October 1952, 40+42

————— "Book Reviews", *Composer*, No.38 (Winter 1970-1971), 30-31

————— "Chto vyrazhaet muzyka?", *Sovetskaya Muzyka*, 29 (January 1965), 5-9

————— "The Composer and Criticism", Alan Bush Music Trust Website

————— "The Composer and His Audience", *London Philharmonic Post*, 4 (July-August 1949), 4-5

————— "Composer's Forum", *Musical Events*, 20 (July 1965), 13

————— "Composer's Forum", *Musical Events*, 24 (July 1969), 24-5

————— [Contribution to] The Caudwell Discussion, *The Modern Quarterly*, 6 No.3 (Summer 1951), 259-62

————— "The Crisis of Modern Music", *Keynote*, 1 (4), Summer 1946, 4-7

————— "Dni muzyki SSSR", *Sovetskaya Muzyka*, 37 (August 1973), 132-3

————— "Eugene Onegin" [Tchaikovsky], *Opera*, 3 No.5 (May 1952), 269-72+316

————— "Festival for Leipzig's new Opera House", *Music and Musicians*, 9 (December 1960), 16-17+

————— Forward [as chairman and founder of the newly-formed William Morris Society], *William Morris Musical Society Bulletin*, No.1 (July 1941), 2

————— "From One of the Victims" [Letter about the BBC ban], *Picture Post*, 10 (22 March 1941), 37

————— (editor) *Handbook of Soviet Musicians* (I. Boelza). London Pilot Press, 1943

————— *In My Eighth Decade and Other Essays*. London, Kahn & Averill, 1980

————— Introduction, in E. Lendvai, *Bela Bartok: An Analysis of His Music*. London, Kahn & Averill, 1971

———— "An Introduction to the Music of Andrew Byrne", *Musical Times*, 103 (July 1962), 456-8

———— "Dmitri Kabalevsky", *The Listener*, 32 No.813 (10 August 1944), 165

———— Letter: "Ansermet on Music: A Forgotten Masterpiece", *Composer*, No. 56 (Winter 1976-1977), 31-2

———— "Music and Life" [Opinions re communism and music], *Musical Opinion*, 79 (May 1956), 453-4

———— "Music and the People", *Music and Musicians*, 5, (October 1956), 11

———— "Music in the British Co-operative Movement", *Bulletin of the Co-operative Education Secretaries' Association*, July 1952, 3-5

———— "Music in the Soviet Union", London, Workers' Music Association, 1944

———— "Musical Education", *The Anglo-Soviet Journal*, 1 No.2 (April 1940), 164-7

———— "Musical Life in the USSR", *The Listener*, 30 No.755 (1 July 1942), 25

———— "My Studies and Friendship with John Ireland", Alan Bush MusicTrust Website

———— "Opera in the USSR", *Opera*, 2, No.5 (April 1951), 218-27

———— "Our President's Greeting", *Vox Pop*, 2 No. 1 (January 1945), 6+10

———— "The Outlook for the British Composers", *The Author*, 52 No.4 (1942), 63-5

———— "Problems of Opera", *Music*, 1 No.11 (October 1952), 19-21

———— "Problems of Soviet Musical Theory", *The Modern Quarterly*, 5 No.1 (Winter 1949/1950), 38-47

———— "A Remarkable Document", *Anglo Soviet Journal*, 10 No.3 (Autumn 1949), 19-20

———— "The 2nd Congress of Composers and Music Critics", *Musical Times*, 89 (September 1948), 280-81

———— "Shostakovitch and his Symphonies", *The Listener*, 27 No.699 (4 June 1942), 733

———— "Some Thoughts about my Chamber Music", Alan Bush Music Trust Website (1981)

———— "Stara Zagora", *Opera*, 26 (July 1975), 647-9

———— *Strict Counterpoint in Palestrina Style – A Practical Textbook.* London, Williams, 1948

———— "The Study and Teaching of Musical Composition", *Musical Times*, 93 (December 1952), 539-42

———— "Tasks of Cultural Workers", *Communist Review*, February 1951, 49-55

———— Tribute to Michael Tippett, in I. Kemp (ed.), *Michael Tippett: A Symposium on his 60th Birthday*. London, Faber & Faber, 1965, 39

———— "The Vocal Compositions of Michael Head", in N. Bush, *Michael Head, Composer, Singer, Pianist: A Memoir*. London, Kahn & Averill, 1982

———— "Wat Tyler and the Purpose of Opera", *Opera*, 25 (June 1974), 488-91

———— "Western Music Today", *Musical Times*, 80 (May 1939), 346 (Reprinted from *Sovetskaya Muzyka*, December 1938)

———— and N. "Twenty-one Years of the Composers' Guild", *Composer*, No. 16 (July 1965), 22-3

———— and Dean, W. "Handel in Halle", *Opera*, 27 (Autumn 1976), 97-104

———— and Roxburgh, E. "John Cage: Letters to the Editor", *Composer*, No.32 (Summer 1969), 32-3

Bush, N. *Alan Bush: Music, Politics and Life*. London, Thames Publishing, 2000

———— "Writing for Music", Alan Bush Music Trust Website. First published in Stevenson, R. (ed.), *Time Remembered – Alan Bush: an 80th birthday symposium*. Kidderminster, Bravura Publications, 1981, 141-6

C., J.O. "London Concerts: Pupils of Alan Bush", *Musical Times*, 94 (March 1953), 129-31

Christiansen, R. "Alan Bush: Obituary", *The Independent*, 3 November 1995, 22

Clark, E. "Foreword", in WMA, Tribute to Alan Bush on his 50th birthday: a symposium. London, WMA, 1950, 11-12

Cole, H. and Amis, J. "Marx and the Music of Time" [obituary], *The Guardian*, 3 November 1995, 15

Croft, A. *Comrade Heart: A Life of Randall Swingler*. Manchester, Manchester University Press

Dalgleish, P. "The Neglected Country", *Musical Opinion*, 124 (March 2001), 82-3

Drew, D. "Man and People", *New Statesman*, 10 December 1960, 921-2

Eisler, H. "...A genuinely progressive man...", in WMA, Tribute to Alan Bush on his 50th birthday: a symposium. London, WMA, 1950, 25

Evans, E. "The Food of Love", *The Sketch*, 8 November 1939, 184

'Feste' "Ad Libitum", *Musical Times*, 83 (September 1942), 275-7

Ford, C. "Burning Bush", *The Guardian*, 8 June 1974, 10

Foreman, L. "Alan Bush at 90", *Musical Times*, 131 (December 1990), 647-8

———— "Alan Bush: Symphonies 1 and 2 a personal exploration", *Clarion*, 7 (2004-2005), [1-3]

———— "Spanning the Century: the Music of Alan Bush", in N. Bush, *Alan Bush: Music, Politics and Life*. London, Thames, 2000

Gill, R. "Composers of Today: 6 Alan Bush", *Our Time*, September 1946, 31

Goddard, S. "Alan Bush: Propagandist and Artist", *The Listener*, 71 No.1830 (23 April 1964), 697

Hall, D. *A Pleasant Change from Politics*, Cheltenham, New Clarion Press, 2001

Hardy, L. *The British Piano Sonata 1870-1945*. Woodbridge, Boydell Press, 2001, 93-5, 175-8

Harrison, M. "Bush at 90", *Musical Times*, 132 (April 1991), 206

Hartley, W.S. "An American composer's tribute", in Stevenson, R. (ed.), *Time Remembered – Alan Bush: an 80th birthday symposium*. Kidderminster, Bravura Publications, 1981, 14

Head, M. "Alan Bush as a fellow student", in Stevenson, R. (ed.), *Time Remembered – Alan Bush: an 80th birthday symposium*. Kidderminster, Bravura Publications, 1981, 69

Henderson, R. "Detecting the Strains of Marxism", *The Daily Telegraph*, 18 January 1986, 9

Hildebrandt, E. "A student friendship in Berlin", in Stevenson, R. (ed.), *Time Remembered – Alan Bush: an 80th birthday symposium*. Kidderminster, Bravura Publications, 1981, 70-73

Hinson, C. "A composer's daughter reminisces", in Stevenson, R. (ed.), *Time Remembered – Alan Bush: an 80th birthday symposium*. Kidderminster, Bravura Publications, 1981, 139-40

Hinson, M. Bush's Chamber Music in Focus", *Clarion*, 4 (2001-2002), [1]

Horrocks, J. "Alan Bush and the WMA: The Later Years", in Stevenson, R. (ed.), *Time Remembered – Alan Bush: an 80th birthday symposium*. Kidderminster, Bravura Publications, 1981, 84-8

Howes, F.S. "Music and Politics", *The Listener*, 25 No.646 (29 May 1941), 781

Jacobs, D. "Alan Bush", *Canon*, 3 No.4 (April 1950), 521

Jacobs, P. "Recording Alan Bush's Piano Music", Alan Bush Music Trust Website (reprinted form the *BMS Newsletter*)

Jemnitz, A. [Message], in WMA, Tribute to Alan Bush on his 50th birthday: a symposium. London, WMA, 1950, 13

Jenner, S. "The Alan Bush Centenary Concerts". Alan Bush Music Trust Website (reprinted from the *BMS Newsletter*)

Jones, M. "Time Remembered", *British Music*, 22 (2000), 30-38

Jordan, J. "Alan Bush (1900-1995): Centenary Concert, *Clarion*, 4 (2001-2002), [7]

Kabalevsky, D. [Message], in WMA, Tribute to Alan Bush on his 50th birthday: a symposium. London, WMA, 1950, 13

Keefe, B. "A View from the Rostrum", in Stevenson, R. (ed.), *Time Remembered – Alan Bush: an 80th birthday symposium.* Kidderminster, Bravura Publications, 1981, 19-20

Keller, H. Bush's "Creative Character", 85th Birthday Concert Programme (January 1986), 5-7 (Reprinted from Stevenson, R. (ed.), *Time Remembered – Alan Bush: an 80th birthday symposium.* Kidderminster, Bravura Publications, 1981, 11-13)

Kotlyarov, B. "Alan Bush", *Sovetskaya Muzyka*, No. 5 (May 1983), 108

———— *Alan Bush*. Moscow, Sovetsky Kompozitor, 1981

———— "Alan Bush: his Soviet biographer's assessment", in Stevenson, R. (ed.), *Time Remembered – Alan Bush: an 80th birthday symposium.* Kidderminster, Bravura Publications, 1981, 21-5

———— "Kompozitor i grazhdanin", *Sovetskaya Muzyka*, 39 (December 1975), 134-9

Leichentritt, H. "Musical Notes from Abroad: Berlin", *Musical Times*, 71 (January 1930), 77

Lyle, W. "Alan Dudley Bush", *The Musical Standard*, 31 No.532 (11 February 1928), 45

MacDonald, C. "Bush at 75", *Tempo*, No. 116 (March 1976), 45

MacDonald, M. "The Music to One pair of Ears", in Stevenson, R. (ed.), *Time Remembered – Alan Bush: an 80th birthday symposium.* Kidderminster, Bravura Publications, 1981, 26-31

McNaught, W. "London Concerts: Soviet Music", *Musical Times*, 81 (May 1940), 227

Mason, C. "Alan Bush", in *Grove's Dictionary of Music and Musicians* (5th edn.), London, Macmillan, 1954, vol. 1, 1037-40 Supplement (vol. 10) published 1961, 54

———— "Alan Bush and the Search for a National Style" *The Guardian*, 1 December 1960, 8

————. "Alan Bush in High Middle Age", *The Listener*, 63 No.1626 (26 May 1960), 954

———— and Cole, H. "Alan Bush", in *The New Grove Dictionary of Music and Musicians*. London, Macmillan, 1980, vol. 3, 502-3

————, Cole, H. and Watson, D. "Alan Bush", in *The New Grove Dictionary of Music and Musicians*. London, Macmillan, 2001, vol. 4, 656-8

Mayer, R. [Message], in WMA, Tribute to Alan Bush on his 50th birthday: a symposium. London, WMA, 1950, 13

Mellers, W. "A Note on Alan Bush and the English Tradition" in WMA, Tribute to Alan Bush on his 50th birthday: a symposium. London, WMA, 1950, 21-4. (Reprinted on the Alan Bush Music Trust Website)

———— "Recent Trends in British Music", *Musical Quarterly*, 38 No.2 (April 1952), 185-201

Meyer, E. "Alan Bush", *Our Time*, May 1948, 206-7

Meyer, E.H. "Alan Bush in the Thirties", in Stevenson, R. (ed.), *Time Remembered – Alan Bush: an 80th birthday symposium*. Kidderminster, Bravura Publications, 1981, 74-5

———— "The Choral Works", in WMA, Tribute to Alan Bush on his 50th birthday: a symposium. London, WMA, 1950, 32-4

Morgan, D. "Artist, Teacher and Friend", in Stevenson, R. (ed.), *Time Remembered – Alan Bush: an 80th birthday symposium*. Kidderminster, Bravura Publications, 1981, 132-3

Murrill, H. "The Teacher", in WMA, Tribute to Alan Bush on his 50th birthday: a symposium. London, WMA, 1950, 17-19

O'Higgins, R. *The Correspondence of Alan Bush and John Ireland, 1927-1961*. Aldershot, Ashgate Publishing, 2006

———— "Dear Alan: Dear John", *Clarion*, 8 (2005-2006), 5

———— "A Journey to Guyana", in Stevenson, R. (ed.), *Time Remembered – Alan Bush: an 80th birthday symposium*. Kidderminster, Bravura Publications, 1981, 136-8

———— "Rhapsody in Red", Alan Bush Music Trust Website

Orga, A. "Alan Bush: Musician and Marxist" *Music and Musician*, 17 (August 1969), 20-22. Reprinted in: *Composer*, No.35 (Spring 1970), 3-4

———— "The Concertos", in Stevenson, R. (ed.), *Time Remembered – Alan Bush: an 80th birthday symposium*. Kidderminster, Bravura Publications, 1981, 45-68

Parfrey, R. "Night-school Composer", *Composer*, No.31 (Spring 1969), 17-19

Payne, A. "Alan Bush", *Musical Times*, 105 (April 1964), 263-5

Rebling, E. [Message], in WMA, Tribute to Alan Bush on his 50th birthday: a symposium. London, WMA, 1950, 14

Riegger, W. [Message], in WMA, Tribute to Alan Bush on his 50th birthday: a symposium. London, WMA, 1950, 14

Ringrose, C. "Bush and the WMA: The Early Years", in Stevenson, R. (ed.), *Time Remembered – Alan Bush: an 80th birthday symposium*. Kidderminster, Bravura Publications, 1981, 80-83

Ross, P. "The Younger English Composers: ix – Alan Bush", *Monthly Musical Record*, 59 (1 October 1929), 289-91

Rostal, M. "A Violin Virtuoso's Collaboration", in Stevenson, R. (ed.), *Time Remembered – Alan Bush: an 80th birthday symposium*. Kidderminster, Bravura Publications, 1981, 116

——— "The Violin Works", in WMA, Tribute to Alan Bush on his 50th birthday: a symposium. London, WMA, 1950, 35-9

Sahnow, W. "Our President", in WMA, Tribute to Alan Bush on his 50th birthday: a symposium. London, WMA, 1950, 26-31

Schafer, M. "Alan Bush", in *British Composers in Interview*. London, Faber & Faber, 1963, 53-63

Schuttenhelm, T. (ed.), *Selected Letters of Michael Tippett*. London, Faber, 2005, 89, 99, 120-39, 220

Schwinger, E.K. "Klingendes Portraet zum 80. Geburstag von Alan Bush", *Musik und Gesellschaft*, 30 (December 1980), 738-9

Scott, E.V. "Alan Bush: Composer", *Hertfordshire County Guide*, March 1969, 35

Schneerson, G. "Alan Bush – rovesnik veka", *Sovetskaya Muzyka*, 34 (December 1970), 123-7

——— "Alanu Bushu 60 let", *Sovetskaya Muzyka*, 25 (January 1961), 190-91

——— "My friend Alan Bush: A Soviet Musicologist's Tribute", in Stevenson, R. (ed.), *Time Remembered – Alan Bush: an 80th birthday symposium*. Kidderminster, Bravura Publications, 1981, 76-9

——— "Nash drug Alan Bush", *Sovetskaya Muzyka*, 29 (November 1965), 122-30

Steptoe, R. "Alan Bush Remembered", Alan Bush Music Trust Website

Stevens, B. "The Choral Music", in Stevenson, R. (ed.), *Time Remembered – Alan Bush: an 80th birthday symposium*. Kidderminster, Bravura Publications, 1981, 32-5

——— "Personal Recollections", in Stevenson, R. (ed.), *Time Remembered – Alan Bush: an 80th birthday symposium*. Kidderminster, Bravura Publications, 1981, 117-18

Stevenson, R. "Alan Bush: Committed Composer", *Music Review*, 25, No.4 (1964), 323-42

——— "Alan Bush: Marxist Musician", *Performance*, 2 (Spring 1981), 44-5

——— "Alan Bush: Obituary", *Tempo*, No. 195 (January 1996), 19

——— "Alan Bush in the 70s", *Musical Times*, 113 (July 1972), 661-3

——— "Bush's Piano Music", in Stevenson, R. (ed.), *Time Remembered – Alan Bush: an 80th birthday symposium*. Kidderminster, Bravura Publications, 1981, 36-44

———— (ed.) *Time Remembered – Alan Bush: an 80th birthday symposium*. Kidderminster, Bravura Publications, 1981

Tippett, M. "A Magnetic Friendship: An Attraction of Opposites", in Stevenson, R. (ed.), *Time Remembered – Alan Bush: an 80th birthday symposium*. Kidderminster, Bravura Publications, 1981, 9

Vaughan Williams, R. [Message], in WMA, Tribute to Alan Bush on his 50th birthday: a symposium. London, WMA, 1950, 14

Wallis, N. "Left Pageants in Britain 1934-44: Preliminaries to a contextual study". BA dissertation in drama, University of Manchester, March 1985

Watson, D. "A Former Student's Tribute", in Stevenson, R. (ed.), *Time Remembered – Alan Bush: an 80th birthday symposium*. Kidderminster, Bravura Publications, 1981, 134-5

Weissmann, J.S. "A Concert of the Compositions of Alan Bush", *Musical Events*, 17 (February 1962), 30-31

Wilson, C. "More 'Brandy of the Damned'", in Stevenson, R. (ed.), *Time Remembered – Alan Bush: an 80th birthday symposium*. Kidderminster, Bravura Publications, 1981, 15-18

Workers' Music Association. Tribute to Alan Bush on his 50th birthday: A symposium. London, WMA, 1950

Classified index of works

Ballet

His War or Yours (1935)
Men and Machines (1934)
Mining (1935)

Brass, Military and Wind Band

(The) Cutty Wren
Dance Overture (Opus 12)
Fanfares [for brass] (1943)
Fantasia on Soviet Themes (1942)
Festival March for British Youth (Opus 78)
Nottingham Fanfares (1949)
Pavane for the Castleton Queen (Opus 43)
Prologue for a Worker's Meeting (Opus 16)
Russian Glory (Opus 20)
Scherzo (Opus 68)

Chamber

Concertino for two violins and piano (Opus 94)
Dialectic for string quartet (Opus 5)
Meditation and Scherzo for double bass and piano (Opus 93 No. 2)
Octet (Opus 105)
Phantasy in C minor for violin and piano (Opus 3)
Pro Pace et Felicitate for cello and piano (Opus 89)

171

Quartet for piano, violin, viola and cello (Opus 5)
Quartet for strings in A minor (Opus 4)
Quintet for piano and strings (Opus 104)
Septet (Opus 118)
Serenade for string quartet (Opus 70)
Serenade and Dance for violin and piano (Opus 111)
Sonata for cello and piano (Opus 120)
Sonata in E minor for violin and piano
Sonata in G for violin and piano
Sonatina for viola and piano (Opus 88)
Song and Dance for violin and piano (Opus 117)
Suite for Six (Opus 81)
Voices from Four Continents (Opus 91)

Choral

Africa is my name (Opus 85)
Against the People's Enemies
(The) Alps and Andes of the Living World (Opus 66)
Ballad of Aldermaston
(The) Ballad of Freedom's Soldiers (Opus 44)
(A) Bridge to the Right
Britain's Part
The Dream of Llewelyn ap Gruffydd (Opus 35)
During Music (Opus 62)
The Earth Awakening
Earth has Grain to Grow
The Earth in Shadow (Opus 102)
For the People's Use
Four Faces of a People
Freedom on the March (1943)
The Great Red Army
It's up to us
Labour's Song of Challenge
Learning to talk
Lidice
Like Rivers Flowing
Make your meaning clear
Mandela Speaking (Opus 110)
March of the Workers

Men of Felling (Opus 72)
My Paper
Nicht den tod aus der Ferne
Once is Enough
Our Song
(The) People's Day
(The) People's Paper
Prisoners (1939)
Question and Answer
Red Front
The Road (Opus 13)
Shining Vision: A Song of Peace
Song for Angela Davis (Opus 75)
Song of Friendship (Opus 34)
Song of the Age
Song to the Commons of England (1944)
Song of the Cosmonaut
Song of the Engineers
Song of the Hunger Marchers
Song of the Men of England (Opus 10)
Song of the Peace-Lovers
Songs of Asian Struggle
Song to Freedom
Song to Labour
(The) tide that will never turn
Till right be done
Toulon
Turkish Workers' Marching Song (Opus 101)
Unite and be Free
The Winter Journey (Opus 29)
Workmates, We must Fight and Strive
A World for Living
The World is his Song (Opus 51)
You Have Betrayed Our Friends

Film Music

Hiroshima
Fifty Fighting Years

Incidental Music

The Duke in Darkness (1947)
Macbeth (1947)
The Star turns Red (1940)

Instrumental Music

Autumn Poem for horn and piano (Opus 45)
Canzona (Opus 106)
Compass Points: Suite for pipes (Opus 83)
Concert Piece for cello and piano (Opus 17)
Corentyne Kwe-Kwe (Opus 75)
Distant Fields for piano (Opus 109)
Duo Sonatina for recorders and piano (Opus 82)
80th Birthday Tribute to Sir Arthur Bliss for piano (1971)
Esquisse: Le 14 Juillet (Opus 38)
Five Pieces of violin, viola, cello, clarinet and horn (Opus 6)
A Hearts's Expression for Piano (Opus 121)
Letter Galliard (Opus 80)
Lively Minuet
Lyric Interlude (Opus 26)
Mister Playford's Tune for piano (Opus 49)
Nocturne for piano (Opus 46)
On Lawn and Green (Opus 54)
Prelude, Air and Dance (Opus 61)
Prelude and Concert Piece for organ (Opus 116)
Prelude and Fugue for piano (Opus 9)
Pricilla's Pavane for cello and piano
Relinquishment for piano (Opus 11)
Round the World for cello and piano
Scots Jigganspiel (Opus 95)
Serenade and Duet for violin and piano (Opus 111)
The Six Modes for Piano Duet (Opus 119)
Six Short Pieces for piano (Opus 99)
Sonata for organ (Opus 118)
Sonata No. 1 in B minor for piano (Opus 2)
Sonata No. 2 in A flat for piano (Opus 71)
Sonata No. 3 in G for piano (Opus 113)
Sonata No. 4 for piano (Opus 119)

Sonata [No. 5] for piano
(A) Song from the North for piano (Opus 97)
Song Poem and Song Dance (Opus 109)
Suite for organ (Opus 117)
Suite for two pianos (Opus 65)
Suite in English Style (Opus 79)
Summer Fields and Hedgerows (Opus 100)
Summer Valley for cello and piano (Opus 125)
Theme for organ (1936)
Three African Sketches for flute and piano (Opus 55)
Three Concert Pieces for piano, violin and cello (Opus 31)
Three Contrapuntal Studies for violin and viola (Opus 13)
Three English Song Preludes for organ (Opus 40)
Three Northumbrian Impressions for pipes (Opus 42)
Three Pieces 'for Nancy' for piano (Opus 115)
Three Pieces for two pianos (Opus 1)
Three Râga Melodies (Opus 59)
Trent's Broad Reaches (Opus 36)
Twenty-four Preludes for piano (Opus 84)
Two Ballads of the Sea (Opus 50)
Two Dances for cimbalom (Opus 64)
Two Easy Pieces for cello
Two Etudes for piano (Opus 118)
Two Melodies for violin and piano (Opus 47)
Two Occasional Pieces for organ (Opus 56)
Two Pieces for piano (Opus 118)
Two Preludes and Fugues for piano (Opus 118)
Two Preludes and Fugues for violin and piano (Opus 108)
Variations on an original theme for piano

Music for Children

The Ferryman's Daughter (1964)
The Press Gang (1946)
Song and Dance for Junior String Orchestra (Opus 96)
The Spell Unbound (1955)
Three Easy 5-beat First Year Pieces for piano (Opus 114)
Time of Day: Four Piano Pieces

Opera

Joe Hill: The Man who Never Died
(The) Last Days of Pompeii
Men of Blackmoor
The Sugar Reapers
Wat Tyler

Orchestral

Africa (Opus 73)
Concert Overture for an Occasion (Opus 74)
Concert Suite for cello and orchestra (Opus 37)
Concerto for piano and orchestra (Opus 18)
Concerto for violin and orchestra (Opus 32)
Dance Overture
Defender of the Peace (Opus 39)
Dorian Passacaglia and Fugue (Opus 52)
English Suite (Opus 28)
Fantasia on Soviet Themes (Opus 24)
Festal Day (Opus 23)
Festival March for chamber orchestra (1922)
For a Festal Occasion (Opus 58)
Homage to William Sterndale Bennett (Opus 27)
The Liverpool Overture (Opus 76)
Meditation for Orchestra in Memory of Anna Ambrose
Meditation on a German Song of 1848 (Opus 22)
Partita Concertante (Opus 63)
Piers Plowman's Day (Opus 30)
Resolution (Opus 25)
Song and Dance for string orchestra and piano (Opus 96)
Symphonic Impression (Opus 8)
Symphony No. 1 (Opus 21)
Symphony No. 2 (Nottingham) (Opus 33)
Symphony No. 3 (Byron) (Opus 53)
Symphony No. 4 (Lascaux) (Opus 98)
Time Remembered (Opus 67)
Variation – Allegro Molto (1955)
Variation, Nocturne and Finale on an English Sea-Song (Opus 60)

Pageants

Communist Manifesto Centenary Meeting and Pageant (1948)
Festival of Music for the People (1939)
The Living English (1946)
Pageant of Co-operation (1938)
The Pageant of Labour (1934)

Songs

Cradle Song for an Unwanted Child
De Plenos Poderes (Opus 86)
Four Seafarers' Songs (Opus 57)
Freedom on the Air (1940)
(The) Freight of Harvest (Opus 69)
Joseph's Narration (1946)
Life's Span (Opus 77)
Peace and Prosperity
The Prison Cycle (Opus 19)
Songs of the Doomed (Opus 14)
Two Shakespeare Sonnets (Opus 92)
Two Songs (Yeats)
Two Songs for Soprano and Chamber Orchestra (Opus 7)
Voices of the Prophets (Opus 42)
Woman's Life (Opus 87)

General index